Breaking the Silence: Voices of Survivors Vol. 2

Curated By
Michelle Jewsbury

Breaking the Silence: Voices of Survivors Vol. 2

Curated By Michelle Jewsbury

Published through:
Amazon/ KDP Select

Copyright © 2024 Michelle Jewsbury Speaks, LLC.

All rights reserved. No part of this publication may be reproduced or transmitted in any form or by any means, graphic, electronic or mechanical, including photocopying, recording, taping or information storage and retrieval systems, without written permission from the author.

ISBN: 9798340234728
Imprint: Independently published

Editor: Jim Martyka
Cover design: Daniel Eyenegho

First printing: 2024
Printed in the United States of America

AUTHOR NOTE

Some names, dates, and locations have been changed in these stories for the authors' protection.

TABLE OF CONTENTS

Foreword by Al Denson

Introduction: *After Escaping* – Michelle Jewsbury   1

Chapter 1: *Seeking Gratitude* – April Blake   6
Chapter 2: *Daring to Believe You Matter* – Sue Bowles   17
Chapter 3: *The Path to Peace* – Michelle Turnbull   28
Chapter 4: *Navigating Grief* – Tami Imlay   38
Chapter 5: *The Journey Within the Journey Begins*
     – Trent Brock   47
Chapter 6: *The Dark Light in Me* – Jaclyn Jereczek   59
Chapter 7: *Becoming the Woman I Came Here to Be*
     – Jennifer Pearce   69
Chapter 8: *The Weight of Whispers* – Kandiee Campbell   79
Chapter 9: *It Runs in the Family* – Leah Hallman   88
Chapter 10: *One in Six* – Andrew Cook   99
Chapter 11: *The Snipers We Couldn't See* – Karen Comba   110
Chapter 12: *Lost and Found* – Annmarie Entner   120
Chapter 13: *Life After Death* – Barry Rothstein   130
Chapter 14: *The Warrior Within* – Beverly Hatfield   140
Chapter 15: *Unheard Screams* – Lisa J. Crawford   150
Chapter 16: *Lucky* – Rebecca Binny   160
Chapter 17: *The Many Stories of Survival* – Jennifer Dall   170
Chapter 18: *Surviving the Decisions and Outcomes*
     – Vivian E. Lopez   180
Chapter 19: *Domestic Violence from the Child's Perspective*
     – Tierra Carter   188
Chapter 20: *Complex*
     – Wah Wah Tas See (Anonymous Author)   197

Epilogue by Michelle Jewsbury   209

FOREWORD

Al Denson

I don't know of a single person who hasn't felt the world collapse around them. In my forty-plus years of being in ministry, I have not only seen and heard about the traumas of others, but I have gone through them myself. In 1994, I was in a plane crash and was lucky to survive. I had broken bones all over my body including a broken back and my nose was completely gone. I was told I would never be able to sing again or even walk. The pilot, who was a friend of mine, died in the accident. When I was forty years old, my big brother died suddenly of a stroke and the loss made me struggle more emotionally than even the plane accident. In 2021, I had a heart attack and required immediate triple bypass surgery that due to some pre-existing health conditions was extremely high risk. I could go on and on with the major traumatic events that I have experienced in my life and I am sure you could, too. The way I got through—and continue to get through—these things today is by the grace of God alone. The ways He shows me His love, strength and support is something I don't deserve but He freely gives it, in both the good and bad times.

Someone once told me you are always in one of three places in life: you are either in the middle of a storm, you just got out of one, or you are about to go into one. The point is life is full of storms and we need to learn how to respond, cope, and heal from them. I have found when you trust God during a storm that once it is over, you truly realize He did not abandon you. And He never will. Our faith is tested the most during these storms.

I believe one of the greatest ways God reminds us of His love for us is to put people in our lives that encourage, support and empathize with us. That is what Michelle Jewsbury is doing through this collection of real-life success stories of people who have not only survived trauma but have come out stronger on the other side. Their resilience is inspiring and it makes me want trust God more so I can be stronger when I am faced with adversity. I don't want to be defined by my past traumas; I want to be known by the way I overcame them. God created us to be overcomers, not victims.

One of my favorite scriptures is 1 Corinthians 10:13 which says, "No temptation has overtaken you except what is common to mankind. And God is faithful; he will not let you be tempted beyond what you can bear." Common to mankind. That alone gives me comfort knowing that other people have struggled with the same things I have. To top it off, God will not give us more than we can handle. Sometimes we don't know what we can truly handle until we are put in the middle of it. But hear me when I say that you are stronger than you think. Whatever you are going through, you are not the first person to deal with it, and you won't be the last. My hope for this book is that you will realize that and be encouraged; and perhaps you will even be inspired to share *your* story with other people as well!

ABOUT THE AUTHOR

Al Denson has one of the most varied, entrepreneurial backgrounds of anyone you will ever meet. His exceptional drive and passion have led him to be successful in many areas. For over thirty years, Al was a recording artist in contemporary Christian music. He toured as a solo artist and performed steadily for many years, playing nightly to crowds of ten thousand-plus. He has had nineteen songs on the Christian radio charts, with eleven of those hitting the number one spots. He is a Dove Award-winning artist.

Al also provided curriculum to schools and teen events across the country for many years, doing motivational speaking in public forums with the invitation to come to a free concert that night, crossing a tough road into non-secular audiences. He hosted his own TV show called *The Al Denson Show* geared toward teens that featured guests and ran for three seasons. He was a consultant for ten years on Disney's "Night of Joy," a massive annual Christian festival held in Disney parks. In 2010, he launched the Experience Conference, an annual event for worship leaders held at Disney World which is still going strong in 2024, now branching out to different markets this coming year as well.

Currently Al is a busy entrepreneur where in addition to being involved in music and worship, he serves on various company and nonprofit boards, is co-owner of eight assisted living facilities, a Hilton Garden Inn, a Cowboy Chicken restaurant franchise and is the founder/president of Wyldewood Homes, a single-family new home construction company in North Texas. He also owns Willowood Ranch, a 350 plus-acre ranch, retreat center, and wedding venue in North Texas. The ranch has also hosted large-scale music festivals including Passion One Day and Lifelight. Willowood Ranch is the definition of a passion project and Al has many plans for its development and growth, including an equestrian arena and lodge.

Breaking the Silence

INTRODUCTION

AFTER ESCAPING

Michelle Jewsbury

When I was a little girl, I would daydream about a perfect love. I remember watching movies like *Snow White* and *Sleeping Beauty,* movies that ended with a prince that came to rescue a damsel in distress. I wanted that. I wanted to be loved.

My childhood was not bad by any means. My parents were middle class, forging their way through life. My daddy, Bill, was a fun-loving, hard-working military man. He served over thirty years with the U.S. Army. I remember some days he would get off work and throw a baseball to my brother and me. I typically missed and had to chase the ball through the prickly brush by our house. I became a gymnast and a cheerleader; this was a better option with my lack of hand-eye coordination.

My brother, on the other hand, excelled in all ball sports. He grew up playing basketball, soccer, baseball, and was even good at bowling. His preference was skateboarding, where he managed to get a sponsor before he was fifteen years old. Unfortunately, my brother had a taste for other things that gave him more of an adrenaline rush, and his career in skateboarding was halted.

My mom was an exceptional woman. Always doing her best to accommodate my brother and me. She worked as a waitress much of her life, saving her tips to pay for our extracurricular activities. She was beautiful, with blonde hair and light blue eyes. She was popular at most of the restaurants she worked at because she excelled in chaos, a trait that she developed as a child.

My mother's life was hard. She grew up in the slums in San Francisco with her mother and four older brothers. She was an unexpected child. Her mother hid the pregnancy until the day she delivered my mom in the hospital. My mother was literally the baby of the family, her youngest brother was eighteen years older than her. Although her brothers loved her, they were trying to live

Breaking the Silence

their own lives, which left her with her non-diagnosed schizophrenic mother.

At the young age of four or five, my mom was left with babysitters while my grandmother tried to make a living. My mom was a very pretty little girl and became a favorite among men in the neighborhood. She began to endure sexual abuse by many different people, and my grandmother either didn't acknowledge what was going on or didn't care.

My mom once told me a story of being in a basement with small windows that opened to the street. She was under the age of ten and began dancing naked in the window. She was isolated, scared, and tried desperately to get someone's attention to stop the violation that seemed to continue throughout the years. Eventually, she and my grandmother moved to a different neighborhood when my grandmother met Bob.

Bob was a financially successful man, a manipulator, and narcissist. Bob and my grandmother were married, but not before he started taking advantage of my mother. He would beat her with hairbrushes, force her to clean incessantly, and regularly molest her. At the age of sixteen, she told my grandmother about the abuse. She replied, "You are lying, Bob would never do such a thing." My mom ran away from home. She moved to Idaho where her oldest brother was. She wanted his protection and guidance. It was in Idaho, when she was nearly eighteen years old, that she met my daddy.

My mom and dad tried very hard through the years to make their marriage work. There is no such thing as perfect, but they were successful in creating a loving home. When my daddy passed away in 2015, my mom couldn't live without him. She didn't know how to survive in a world without her protector, lover, and best friend. She tried to live for my brother and me, but that was not enough to diminish the grief that consumed her. She died in 2019 from a broken heart.

I look back at my parents' love story and understand where my desperate need for romance came from. Growing up, I started dating boys who I thought could be like my daddy. Someone who could take care of me and provide for my emotional and physical

Breaking the Silence

needs. During my adolescence, our family moved frequently to different cities across the U.S. I learned to become a chameleon—able to fit into different friend groups and transform my personality.

I started experimenting with drugs when I was just thirteen years old, thinking this was what the "cool kids" did. Although my parents were loving, they sometimes missed the emotional torment my brother and I went through during our transitions from one school to the next. I excelled in academia, but partied nightly, searching for the right boy to help me find a permanent place I could call home. My brother subconsciously chose to rebel to get attention.

When I graduated high school, I decided the attention I sought after was on the silver screen. I moved to Hollywood when I was nineteen years old to pursue an acting career. Things were going as planned as I was finding favor among casting directors, starring in plays and films, and even producing my own show. Along the way I met someone. A blond-haired, blue-eyed boy who swept me off my feet. He began courting me and sending me gifts and flowers with cards that read, "You are the most beautiful woman I have ever met." I swooned.

He moved me north, wanting to build a life with me. He said he would be my Prince Charming and "take care of me." I was elated with the idea of love. I wanted the fairy tale life I had seen in the movies and the love affair that my parents had. Shortly after moving, the onslaught began.

The first time my head went through the wall was roughly four months into our relationship. I remember arguing with Paul, then suddenly he pushed me so hard that my head made a huge indentation in the drywall. I thought to myself, "I need to patch that," instead of, "I need to run away." I didn't understand the red flags of domestic violence. I didn't see that there was a pattern developing that would continue through the duration of our relationship.

Generational trauma is often overlooked. My mother did all she could to protect me during my teens and early twenties, but I still ended up being attracted to an abuser. To stop generational abuse, survivors need to accept and seek help for what they went through. My mother thought therapists could not help her and she pushed down many of her emotions, not expressing her feelings of neglect and trauma she endured as a child. This led to her crying regularly and giving family and friends the silent treatment when she was upset. Expressing yourself leads to healing and my mother never achieved healing.

    I stayed with Paul for over four years, thinking I could change him. I experienced intense physical, emotional, sexual, and financial abuse. The police were called many times during our relationship, but I always backed away from pressing charges. It wasn't until early 2015 that I finally understood the severe implications on my mental and physical well-being. I escaped the relationship and sued him for the abuse I endured.

    I started to document my experience, which first came out in a play format. I showcased an hour-long solo piece in 2016 about my story entitled, *But I Love Him*. Each night, after the play ended, many people came up to me and told me their stories. All were different, yet the same: intense violence and the silencing of their voice. I felt called to do something even more.

    In 2017, I founded a nonprofit organization called *Unsilenced Voices*. We began in West Africa, expanding from Ghana to Sierra Leone and even did work with partner organizations in Rwanda. In 2022, we gifted $33,000 to U.S. survivors and hosted a four-city tour highlighting the main hubs for human trafficking in the nation: Dallas, Vegas, Los Angeles, and Tampa. In 2022, we published a curriculum called *Graced For Prosperity*, an eight-module training that teaches financial literacy and how to overcome pain and trauma. The digital version can be found at no cost on UnsilencedVoices.org.

    In 2019 I began speaking on stages around the globe. At first, I spoke strictly about my story and the after-effects of abuse. Along this journey, I began to discover my mission was not about Michelle Jewsbury but providing a platform for others to tell their stories. I started developing programs and services to help others tell their stories on stages, through books, and creating courses of their own. I surrounded myself with people who could help me and

Breaking the Silence

I developed a team and created a successful business. Through a service-led heart, dreams can become a reality.

In 2024 we published the first volume of *Breaking the Silence: Voices of Survivors*—a book that was originally designed to give a handful of people an opportunity to publish their experiences. We found that there were so many different stories that needed to be heard. We are committed to providing this platform to authors every year to not only tell their stories but also provide hope and encouragement for readers who are experiencing adversities.

In these next pages, you will read stories from twenty individuals who have experienced grief, trauma, disease, abuse, addiction, suicide, and more. Let their stories inspire you to not stay a victim of circumstance but become a victor in the face of your adversities.

CHAPTER 1

SEEKING GRATITUDE:

WITHOUT LOVE IN A DREAM, IT WILL NEVER COME TRUE

April Blake

I was born to the coolest parents ever. Or was I?

My parents were both spoiled and favorites in their families. My father was raised in a family with little to no morals, no religion, and would defend him at all costs. My mother could do no wrong, raised Mormon, and handed everything. A beautiful disaster. My mom was nineteen and Dad was twenty-one when I was born. I grew up on my dad's Harleys and custom choppers. To this day, when I hear the rumble of a motorcycle, I feel it throughout my bones, bringing me back to good times. I remember riding on my dad's motorcycle, popping wheelies down the street, neighbors calling the cops, me crying and yelling at the cops to not take my daddy to jail.

My dad was amazing, handsome, and talented and everyone knew it. While still in high school, he built a custom chopper for an executive at Columbia Records. Dad was charming, he looked like Robert Redford and just as charismatic. The executive liked him so much, he gave him a job at Columbia Records. We moved to the Bay Area while he worked for Columbia Records. I was an only child and often joined my parents on their adventures, sleeping on my dad's lap during an Eric Clapton concert, and hanging around pre- and post-concert parties with the adults. I always felt safe with him, except when he was mad. I would just slip inside my body, be still, and disappear. That began a lifetime of how to act when *anyone* was angry.

My mom was a five-foot, cute, bubbly little gymnast. Throughout high school, she was adored by everyone. Her parents would do anything for her, although they couldn't afford to do so. They forever tried. When I was born, she was never questioned about when she would drop me off at a relative's house, saying she'll return soon. Minutes turned to hours, hours turned to days. We would hit the drive thru at Taco Bell in her orange convertible

Breaking the Silence

Fiat where she ordered "a Pepsi with a lot of ice," sucking on both the straw of her drink in one hand and her cigarette in the other. She was always nervous and screaming at people when we drove. I was just along for the ride, never talked to, just criticized if I did something wrong. Otherwise, never acknowledged.

In kindergarten, my dad hid a house key for me so that I could get into the house after school. Oftentimes, my mom wasn't home until dinner time. She was angry when she found out my dad hid a key for me. She must have felt so humiliated, her husband checking up on her parenting skills. I wished so many times that I had a sibling to share the chaos with, basically just to confirm, "Am I nuts or is it the crazies around me?"

When I was six, my dad took me to my great-grandmother's funeral, which turned into a six-month abduction. For the funeral, I went to Oklahoma with his mom, a very overweight, miserable, hateful woman who was once a beautiful and extremely talented pianist. I believe she married a monster. What I didn't know was that my mom couldn't find me. My favorite people in my world—my grandparents Gram and Big Tony—found me. They were good people, both worked for the school district and Gram charmed someone to share confidential school information. Big Tony would visit me at school during lunch, where we would play and have fun together. I could never share this type of fun with the other miserable grandparents once I was picked up after school. To this day, I never fully processed why I was with those people and Big Tony never uttered a word of negativity about them. That is true character.

Turns out, Dad was trying to gain custody of me during this time. He promised my mom their entire music collection in exchange for me. She said yes, it was an easy decision. Mom was twenty-five years old, living in the music scene in San Francisco … what could be better! Sounded good to her, but her mother (Gram) would never let that happen. The judge ruled in Gram and Big Tony's favor (and my mom's). I was forced to say goodbye to my dad because I knew I wouldn't see him for a while. That night, I crept into his bedroom and hugged him while he slept. The next day, I was picked up from the grandparents by my mom and her

Breaking the Silence

new boyfriend and dropped off at Gram and Big Tony's house. There was a buzz of laughter and joy as I was back with my favorite people. They knew their happy home was the best place for me. The boyfriend was okay; he was just a big kid. In my mom's eyes, you were only fun if you didn't work. He didn't, and money was always tight. Two weeks into living with my mom, I fell from a three-story balcony, breaking my arm. Gram came to pick me up to stay with her for the remainder of the summer.

In second grade, I was back with my mom and had a really good time in the streets of San Francisco. Our neighborhood was a potpourri of race, income, and culture. My mom's best friend, Aunt Ter, was married to a music executive, and had a boy, Justin, the same age as me. We roamed the streets together. Justin was the best, teaching me a lot, and soon taught me how to hang out with people. He was outgoing and well-liked. I was always super shy and preferred to be out of the spotlight. I was super smart and buried myself in my schoolwork, reading, and music. There were so many things that we saw as kids: mountains of cocaine on coffee tables, watching the adults partaking, including my mom. I was the joint passer while sitting in a circle of neighbors known as "the boys," which was a house of gay guys. They were sweet and kind but look out when they would fight; it sounded like street cats making love.

Aunt Ter lived three houses down, often was a stand-in for my mom. She was sweet, kind, and beautiful. I often wished she was my own mother. She was home more than my own. She made sure I ate, bathed, and went to bed at some point. Fortunately, I was liked by her husband, so I could stay at their house rather than being alone on my own. He would play scrabble with me, take Justin and I to concerts, 49ers and Giants games, and hang out in his record store. We knew we were lucky kids—the perks of the music business were never-ending and always exciting.

By fourth grade, I went to live with Gram and Big Tony and it was the best year. Gram was a secretary at the school I attended, Big Tony was home after school daily ... heaven. My days consisted of Gram cooking dinner while Big Tony and I were together. Often, Gram and I would head out clothes shopping

Breaking the Silence

where she would tell me to keep the bags in the car so Big Tony wouldn't see. I was one of the best-dressed girls at school wearing my Wiggles jeans. In fifth grade, my mom insisted that I join her in San Francisco, as she claimed I was too spoiled by Gram and BigTony. Why? I had a stable home, food, went to a great school, and had amazing friends which equaled spoiled in her mind. That year, I went to four schools. Mom's boyfriend had left. She was a bartender at night. Justin and his family moved to the burbs; the old neighborhood had become quiet. I would come home and play outside for a bit. Our landlord had boys around my age. He was a single dad, a great guy who would take me out to dinner with them as he knew I was alone otherwise. It was embarrassing when they would ask questions about where my mom was. I knew it was wrong, what she was doing, but what could I say? After closing the bar, Mom would come home around 2:30 a.m. Often, bringing "friends" or people who weren't ready to stop drinking at the bar, so the party continued at our house. I would wake up hearing people laughing, crying, and never leaving. By morning, I would wake up on my own, get ready, and go to school on the city bus. I would come home to an empty house, eat dinner by myself or with the landlord, starting the routine over again.

    I finally had enough, packed up my clothes and my cat named "Gram" and took the Greyhound bus to Sacramento. I adopted Gram from someone who had too many cats. My mom told me to name her after someone I really loved, so the cat's name was Gram. How I got my cat on the bus, I'll never know. Once I arrived in Sacramento, I called a friend of my mom and dads who knew where Dad lived. I asked her to pick me up and take me to his house. You see, I hadn't seen or talked to my dad since maybe second grade. I showed up that Friday night, knocking on the door around 9:30. My stepmom answered the door. She was everything my mom wasn't—responsible, family-centric, and she enjoyed being a mom. I stood on the porch as I asked if I could live with them ... with my cat of course. They took me inside where I learned I had a six-month-old baby sister who was sleeping in her crib. Kelly was perfect, so sweet, the best girl. She immediately became my pride and joy.

Breaking the Silence

I was exposed to so many different individuals in my life: my mom was a hippie, a drug addict, a favorite in her family, and a bartender. Dad was indescribable, a biker, hardworking and fun, who thought that living in the city was a form of torture that no one should endure. Gram, born in the Great Depression, a practicing Mormon. Big Tony, first-generation born Portuguese American from the Azores, honest, hardworking, serving his community, president of their homeowner's association, on the school district board for which they worked. Growing up with the Grateful Dead and Deadheads, I learned whimsical kindness and acceptance. Try to imagine the cast of characters—the good, the bad, and the ugly I was exposed to. I am grateful for it all. Today, I can relate to anyone and judge no one. I mastered the art of looking like I had it together although I harbored fear and anxiety. I tried to not be a burden to my family, acting mature for my age, and having no emotional needs. Later, because I had been so mature as a kid, I felt like I was immature as an adult, merely surviving. With my legal background, I have served many children in the Guardian ad Litem program, advocating for the best interest of the child. Throughout my years serving, I realized how close I was to going into the "system," often wondering if that would have made a difference in my outcome.

Whenever our car was broken down on the side of the road, my mom would sit there, stoned, and say, "April, I know you will always take care of me." I was conditioned to believe this was my destiny. As a teenager and older, I never let loose and had fun. What if something happened? Ain't nobody going to bail me out of jail, I had to bail my own mom out!

At twenty-three, I married someone like my dad—hardworking and responsible. I craved a safe, secure life so badly. Nothing like my mom who didn't worry about how to pay next month's rent. Even before we married, I knew exactly what to do just before he got home. I would start the washer and dryer, and dishwasher. That way, he wouldn't be so angry when he walked in the door, for his woman was taking proper care of him and his home. Again, just slip inside my body, be still, and disappear. I was just thinking the other day about that relationship and how I

Breaking the Silence

thought it was normal for certain people to screech through a parking lot, break things, and get angry, like my father and Cameron's father. I had Cameron when I was twenty-three. As a newborn, he would cry at night. I would take him into the living room and whisper for him to be quiet. For if his father awoke, we both would get in trouble. I went to work with bruises on my neck from him choking me. Working full-time, during my lunch hours, I would look for a place to live. Cam was four-months old when I found the courage to leave. I had a friend with a truck come to my house to move me and Cam out. He was standing in the driveway and shouted, "You better send your friend home if you want her to live." I asked her to leave, and I was alone with him yet again. The move was delayed, but I eventually found the courage to leave with nothing but our lives. I understood that material objects were worth nothing as your life can never be replaced.

Around that time O.J. had killed his wife, Nicole, he would call me and leave messages saying, "Nicole, I'm coming to get you …" He would come to my house, breaking furniture, saying, "if I ever called the cops, my throat would be slit before I dialed 911." I persevered, working full-time, raising Cam, and keeping everything to myself because who could I share this disaster with? Karma got that monster, and he killed himself while in jail for a list of things including domestic abuse before Cam turned five.

I met a guy closer to my age—a musician and student—while working part-time. I had been a sucker for musicians since my Grateful Dead days. He was happy and oh so chill. Perfect. We had fun, but he wanted to marry right away. The running joke with my girlfriends was, don't ever ask me to marry you because I can't say no! This was the happiest time in my life. My mom was getting sober, and she lived with us and cared for the kids while I worked. I had Christopher four years after Cam. We were officially a family, one that I had always dreamed of. It was challenging, but so fun. I was content for a bit. I matured and set goals … but he didn't do either. I knew I was destined for more.

My dad did well for himself, with my stepmom always by his side. They were a power couple, great successes, and filled one another's gaps. Their specialty was to buy/sell "fixer" houses, all while working a successful construction company. Their houses were like no other, always fun to watch their magic in motion. It was always hard for any man to compete with Dad. You couldn't compete with him; my sister and I would always laugh at the men who tried.

At the age of thirty-six, I had Lucas. He's the greatest kid ever. I found that with each of my children and their personalities, it truly reflects where I was in my life as a mom! Cam was always nervous as he had a crazy father; Chris was just happy to be alive (remember, that is when I was the happiest in my life). Then along came Lucas, who had to be induced because he was so chill, perfectly comfortable in Momma's tummy. Having children older was so different. I let the boys name Lucas, and they were so excited. Cam was then thirteen and Chris was nine. I was able to parent Lucas in a way that I wasn't when Cam and Chris were little. I was in a good place when Lucas was a baby; learning to meditate, practicing gratitude, letting my spirit grow, and finding my faith. I always believed how important self-care was.

Amongst the chaos and turmoil, I saw the importance of gratitude, eating right, taking care of yourself. Not punishing yourself with booze, cigarettes, and drugs. In parenting, I did the best I knew, while continuing to evolve as my children grew. The main goal I have as a parent is to be there for them emotionally, teaching them how to emotionally regulate, being consistent in my love and support, allowing them to fail while still supporting them.

"Do the best you can until you know better. Then when you know better, do better." -Maya Angelou

I divorced when Lucas was around two, Chris eleven and Cam fifteen. Later, I moved in too soon with my current husband. I think we both see that now. We connected in such a way where we both enjoyed working, working together, and having fun while working. Again, married too soon. One year after we married, River was born. Lucas was thrilled when we told him he was going to be a big brother. Cam's first trip to rehab was when I was

Breaking the Silence

pregnant with River; Cam had his first DUI on River's first Christmas. From then on, my cortisol levels skyrocketed.

Cam had become obsessed with taking care of Gram, becoming very needy since Big Tony passed. I believe that Big Tony kept Gram a good person. When he passed, she reverted to her dark side I never knew. I was a stressed-out mess while trying to raise Chris, Lucas, and River pretending everything was fine with no emotional support from family. I had lost myself, stripping my identity, forgetting my purpose, and what inspired me.

Cam became addicted to Gram's pain pills. Soon after, her physician began to prescribe drugs to Cam directly. Back then, it was easier to get the prescription itself. Eventually becoming more difficult; counterfeits were laced with fentanyl. People were overdosing often. He struggled off and on for years. Due to my own ignorance, I never truly understood why it was so hard for him. He had many demons, yet he was the sweetest, kindest, and most thoughtful child you would know.

During this time, my mom moved from California to North Carolina. I was trying to help her and hoping we could help one another. She watched the boys while I worked. We found a cute loft apartment in our office building, but she couldn't stay sober. A package was mistakenly delivered to our office addressed to her, from a drug buddy in California. I knew in my gut what it was. I held that package for weeks while I heard her complain about our small-town post office. I finally found the courage to confront her. With the package in hand, I knocked on her door. She saw the package and tried to grab it. I said, "We both know what this is and my boys will not be around you and this drug. You can't do that here." She snatched the package from my trembling hand and said, "I guess I'm going back to California then." We never spoke of it again and she soon moved back. My mom could have been and done anything in her life. She was smart, fun, and beautiful. Successful men wanted to marry her, but when meth took a hold of her, it never let go, and she lost everything, including me and my boys.

After my mom left for California and Gram was settled in a residential facility, my boys and I had a great time. We all knew we tried to help my mom. Cam was sober and doing well, we were all close and loved each other. About six months later, Cam relapsed. I awoke that morning feeling off, so I decided to wear a bright shirt to try to lift my spirits. On the way to work, I received a call from Cam's partner. He was a pilot and was out of town frequently. He asked if I had heard from Cam. No, I said I was just going to call him. He told me that he had done a welfare check, and the person said he found Cam in their bathroom. He appeared "expired." I will never forget that word. Being the eternal optimist, I thought that just couldn't be true.

    My first call was to Chris. I remember saying, "I think I need you." I have always been extremely independent and to say that, Chris knew something was very wrong. He was working out of town, so he sent his friend/neighbor AJ, whom I refer to as my fifth son. He came over to be with me, and the police chaplain came, confirming the news, and left. When I was ready to drive to Cam's, my car wouldn't start. It was new, so no reasoning behind it. AJ jumped it and I was off. My cousin drove with me to Cam's. We stopped along the way and my car wouldn't start again. A nice older man jumped it. By the time I arrived at Cam's house, the coroner had just left with Cam's body. I am convinced Cam made sure I wouldn't be at his house when his body was still there because he knew that I shouldn't see that. He was and always is looking out for me.

    Classic Cam story: After Cam's death, I received a call from his mechanic to tell me that while at his shop, Cam witnessed a mom with lots of kids. Her car had barely made it to the shop and everyone was hot, sweaty, and stressed. She was told the cost to repair the car, pay now or take a cab home. Cameron went to the counter and paid the bill. The mom had written a note to him and given it to the mechanic.

    Cam passed in 2017, I struggled and was alone. We fought like crazy, but he was my rock. We had gone through so much together and always were there for one another. He had a best friend in high school, Joanelle. For years after Cam died, Joanelle would visit every Friday. It was such a kind gesture, helping all of us with the healing of losing Cam. Telling Gram about Cam was the hardest thing. I also asked Gram to make sure my mom did not attend the service as she would have caused a scene. After Cam died, I had nothing to say to both my mom and Gram. There were generations of mistrust and buried emotions in our family.

    Struggling to keep it together, I continued to raise my kids; Chris was nineteen, knee-deep in a toxic relationship; Lucas was eleven, heading into the hormonal highs and lows. Cam had a close relationship with Lucas, taking him to museums, hockey, and baseball games. I have not seen Lucas smile as big since Cam died. River was a sweet boy, four just turning five. I had to keep going for my boys and have continued to do so.

    Today I do not want pity. Nor do I have excuses for things that happened to me or things I have done. Losing my child to a drug overdose will not label me. Today I celebrate life because I know how delicate life is. Today I practice gratitude for everything and all the people I have met in this patchwork life, teaching me how to maneuver gracefully. Today I surround myself with beautiful friends because I am no longer in the dysfunction of my family. Today I am here to show you how I have not merely survived but thrived. If I can inspire someone who is going through similar challenges, I have fulfilled my purpose. Today the relationships with each of my boys are as unique as they are, and I love them with all my heart.

    I have never been so excited for the future, feeling like I have finally made it to the other side. I am ready to fully celebrate life, finding gratitude every day for my blessings, waking up ready to smile, talk to strangers, and making their day happier and complete. I have made the conscious decision to no longer have a relationship with my mother. People judge me, but no one knows what it is like to be her daughter.

    This story is not just mine; it belongs to us all. It is my hope that you can relate to your own life, finding strength, and resilience while appreciating a mother's love and loss while reading this chapter. Together, we will break the stigma and silence that surrounds addiction and the mental illness that precedes it.

Breaking the Silence

Join me on a journey of healing and renewal. I have organized a series of retreats designed to offer solace, rejuvenation, and a deeper connection to ourselves. The retreats are set in the breathtaking Azores, feeling like home with a personal connection to Big Tony, whose legacy I cherish deeply. The spirit of the Azores not only provides a stunning location, but each day is filled with Pilates, helping you reconnect with your body, regardless of your experience level. We also explore the natural beauty of the island, engaging in mindful practices that foster inner peace and balance, all while eating delicious food with the welcoming natives of the island. This is a chance to reset your body. If you're seeking healing, vitality or simply a deeper connection within yourself, this adventure provides the space and support you need with an unforgettable week in the Azores. Above all, we will have amazing fun while building our community!

ABOUT THE AUTHOR

April's life is one of profound resilience and unwavering determination. Her early childhood began with divorced parents, a drug-addicted mother, and then she lives through domestic abuse, surviving the tragic loss of her oldest son to a drug overdose.

Learning to navigate life while facing the challenges of breaking the familial cycle of both mental illness and addiction, she is working to make a better life for her boys. Through speaking and writing, she inspires others to embark on a transformative journey of healing and self-discovery, offering solace and understanding to those who experience similar paths of heartache and loss. She has served in the North Carolina Guardian ad Litem program to assist abused and neglected children by advocating for their best interests in court.

Her life is a testament to the power of love, perseverance, and self-acceptance. Driven by a desire to empower others to embrace their own resilience through movement, she is becoming a Pilates instructor, leading others on a path toward fostering strength and inner peace while building community.

Stay in touch: @apple.blake and www.aprilblake.net

CHAPTER 2

DARING TO BELIEVE YOU MATTER

Sue Bowles

"What you're really saying, Sue, is you don't matter."

I sat on the thick-cushioned couch in Amanda's counseling office with a death grip on a throw pillow, my arms clutched around it, guarded, emotional. Gazing down, I raised my eyes over the top of the pillow in a fixed stare at the compassionate tough love look on her face. She sat quietly, letting the words penetrate. Words that stung. They pierced. They silenced. My common cop-out—*"It doesn't matter."*—had been challenged.

If you've read my first book, *This Much I Know…The Space Between* (2019), you've read of Amanda. I didn't know how powerful her words would become in my healing and growth.

Amanda and I started working together in 2008. I sought help when, three years after the death of a dear friend, I was grieving as if it were yesterday. My eating disorder behaviors were activating, and I was not well. Desperate for a change in my life, and in a short time, I committed to being "all in" to fight for my healing. I didn't know what that meant or what we would find. I just needed relief. After a few sessions, feeling despair, I asked her, "What do you think it is? What's causing it all to come back?"

"I think it's bunch of unresolved issues" she replied. So, we got to work.

Amanda had weekly homework assignments for me. In a weird way, I enjoyed them. They gave me permission to start digging into all I had hidden for decades. It was a safe way to share my secrets.

The biggest secret, my trauma, was revealed within the first few sessions. Her first homework assignment for me was to write a "life timeline" of every significant event I could remember. We spent a number of those first sessions going over it—line for line.

My timeline started with age six—winning my dog. The second entry was age seven—first grade, raped by Jason. The absence of my birth on the timeline was a telling sign of my secret belief that I didn't matter.

"I already have questions, but I've looked ahead," Amanda commented, proceeding to read the second entry. Looking up at me, she asked the pivotal question which would pave the road we would later travel.

"Sue, this is huge! Have you ever worked it through with anyone?"

"I wouldn't know what that would look like, so I guess there's your answer." It took six years for us to get me stronger in the present before we could start dealing with the past.

We spent the next several years addressing struggles, especially around boundaries and standing up for myself. I allowed myself to be emotionally manipulated and abused. Without fail, when the emotions got too intense to deal with and I wanted to shut down, I used the "It doesn't matter" cop-out. Amanda would again challenge what I was really saying: *I* didn't matter.

In 2014, over four decades after it happened, we started digging into the rape. Emotions are not the friends of eating disorders. As such, there was an internal war going on to face my story, learn to feel, and not implode in the process. *Ragamuffin,* a movie by Color Green Films about the late Christian musician Rich Mullins, was released earlier in the year. While I saw it numerous times, it was a hard watch as it struck close to home in many ways. Later the same year, the producer, family, and friends of Rich organized a retreat around the themes of the movie— parent/child relationships, living authentically, the masks we wear, and our identity in Christ. Agreeing to attend the retreat was a tug-o-war with God that I finally lost. I struggled with fear of authenticity as I prepared for the retreat when a comment from a family member pierced my armor.

Recently released from serving an eighteen-month prison sentence for a drunk driving accident, a family member saw someone at the store. "I haven't seen you for a while. Where've you been?" his friend innocently asked.

"In prison."

Breaking the Silence

I was struck by this family member's authenticity, boldly owning that chapter of his story. My walls and masks were penetrated. If he could be authentic after just getting out of prison, maybe I, too, could be freed from my forty-year prison sentence.

I relayed the story to Amanda the following week. I had been fighting authenticity too long. With resignation in my voice, I invited her in.

"I just want to be authentic. Get me ready."

We spent the next six weeks leading up to the retreat dealing with my fears, anxieties, hesitations, and hopes laced with doubt. Enough doubt to keep them silent. I had been imploding. Trauma recovery is hard work. I was desperate for relief. I hoped I would experience what it meant to matter to someone, anyone. I didn't realize attending the retreat was telling myself that I mattered.

The retreat hosted a private Facebook group for those attending. As this was the first retreat and the only commonality was the *Ragamuffin* movie, the staff courageously asked us to share our stories in the safety of the room. I lurked in the room, hiding in the shadows of others' stories, commenting and encouraging them, but not sharing my own. A few days later, my nervous heart felt like it was pounding outside my chest, telling me it was my turn. With the liquid courage of hot coffee to fight my fear, I wrote my carefully guarded secret. I took a hard gulp, then hit "post." The rest of the day I feverishly checked the comments, convinced I would hear in one way or another what had been a common theme in my life—that I was a screw-up, and I was to blame for everything. To my surprise, the comments were the exact opposite.

"You're so brave. You give me courage to share my story," and "I can't wait to meet you. Your story inspires me."

My mindset going into the first retreat was being the "holy exception." I'm a Christ-follower, yet I felt disqualified from being able to live freely due to my life experiences. I had bought the lie that I was too screwed up, too far gone, and a total waste of space. A staff member shared that the first retreat was like a "Hail Mary" for me to find the answer to the core question—was I lovable? In short, do I matter?

My walls slowly began to crumble during the retreat. Messages hit with pin-point precision, cutting through the protective fat around my heart to get to the core. My denial, my masks, my fears all led to me not owning my story. I may have talked about it, but I was not emotionally connected to it. By the end of the retreat, and a bucket of tears later, I began telling myself I mattered as I came face-to-face with the harsh reality of my story, the reality I had tried to sugarcoat and deny. By owning my story, I took the foundational first step in moving toward healing.

I returned to the retreat the following year, feeling movement and growth from the first retreat. I was no longer fearful, but nervously curious. Something began to change in me after the first retreat. I found a glimmer of hope. While I still struggled with my masks, I found a place where I was accepted, secrets and all. I was not judged. Instead, I found a group of people who truly cared for and cheered me on. I started developing a sense of belonging and true community. And I wanted more.

Retreat was described in the early years as "open-heart surgery without anesthesia," meaning there was a lot of deep spiritual work in a short period of time. For true transformation to occur, you must face head-on the things you've been avoiding. For me, that meant dealing with the pain and weight of the loss in my story. Daring to believe I mattered looked like grieving my story. Grieving meant feeling the depth of the emotion behind the losses I had endured. I did not allow myself to cry or be fully angry over anything I experienced. I was only beginning to explore my true emotions. Through the process of the retreat, I had a "sacred moment of release" expressed through hard, extended guttural crying, where I was able to let go of the emotional chains that held me captive. All my secret tears had finally been given an escape hatch. My greatest fear was that I would cry and never stop. That fear was realized and dismantled. I cried. I ugly cried. And I stopped. I walked away freer than I had felt up to that point in my life.

Breaking the Silence

I began writing my first book, *This Much I Know...The Space Between* after the retreat, as I started to live in more emotional freedom than I had previously experienced. I believed that my story may help someone else. It was a cathartic, therapeutic process, wrought with fear and doubt. Most in my family didn't know my story, and I was about to blow my cover.

By now, Walking Stick Retreats, the retreat program, had become a priority in my life. I returned to the retreat each year. The growth born from each subsequent retreat became building blocks for Amanda and me. Every year, after each retreat, she and I took an extended session to debrief. After the second retreat, things changed. Amanda moved to South Carolina. If we were to continue working together it would be virtual. While I had other less desirable options in continuing therapy, I chose to wait until Amanda had Grace Recovery Counseling up and running.

It was during this time my life took another unexpected turn. My eating disorder started to ramp up. While Amanda had recommended a dietician a few times, I was successful in dodging the suggestion. Until 2016. Over the course of several weeks, Amanda kept challenging me to see a dietician.

"Is it really that bad?" I asked after a few weeks. My denial was still waging war.

"Yes, it is, Sue."

I eventually relented, and for the first time, I entered true recovery from my eating disorder. Having to learn to eat a balanced diet, coupled with the emotions it brought on, made for a challenging year. I took a year break from book writing. I had no emotional energy other than figuring out this food thing.

My search for healing was catapulted to new levels after the 2016 fall retreat. I had found a community where I belonged, was loved, could be more courageous, and could struggle without fear of rejection. I could safely work at rediscovering who I was and who God created me to be before the stains of the world took over. After two years of hard heart cultivation through retreat and subsequent therapy, the ground of my heart was ready for new thoughts and beliefs to take root. In 2016, I left the retreat with the nugget "I AM valuable to God." And that's when things pivoted.

Breaking the Silence

It was Thanksgiving 2016. I was only four months into my recovery, contending with a food-centric holiday wrought with emotions of every kind. The holiday was a train wreck. Boundaries are resisted by those who are being limited by them. I had little emotional energy to deal with food when I was drained from communicating my needs. Tensions were high as expectations for the day had long been destroyed. I spent much time in my room isolating, crying, trying to withstand the nightmare and make it to the next day, which only added to the stress and emotional upheaval. I just needed to survive. I was texting my dietician who, at one point, called me to offer support and ideas to make it through. I ended up eating a turkey pot pie for dinner. But at least I made it through without giving in to my eating disorder tendencies to only snack and not eat a meal.

At the same time, I was a volunteer with an online eating disorder advocacy group while still struggling with my recovery. We had shifts to offer support for our online community. I unexpectedly found myself helping others who struggled while I needed to lean on my dietician to survive. While it felt odd, it was also empowering. I helped others while still figuring it out in my life. It reminded me of something I had heard at church the year before. Dale, my pastor, was teaching on growth and influencing others.

"What's it take to help the person behind you?" he asked.

Then, answering his own question, he said, "You only have to be a step ahead." Dale's comment landed on my heart

I first heard the phrase "step by step" in a 1991 conversation with a dear friend, Billy Sprague. I was barely holding on when my parents divorced. I was depressed, not eating, and withdrawn. It was the second time I thought about ending my life. Billy shared his story of hanging on after his fiancé had been killed in a car wreck on the way to surprise him. He shared about watching his shoes as he walked, telling himself with each step, "One more step. I'm one step closer. I can do this." Billy's last words to me were, "That's all I know to tell you, Sue. Step by step."

Breaking the Silence

Hearing Dale's comment brought it all back to mind. Thus, the concept of my business, My Step Ahead LLC, was born. Taking Dale's point as a building block on the foundation laid through the retreats, coupled with my experience at Thanksgiving, I began to see the 2016 nugget, "I am valuable to God," come to life. A steady flow of energy and dreams began to come to mind. The thought of having something to offer someone else while I was healing was freeing. Exciting. Liberating. For the first time, I began to believe that I mattered. What I was searching, yearning, and wishing for was beginning to take shape.

My budding belief of having something to offer quickly led to my desire to start speaking. I published my book, which went on to win second place in nonfiction at the 2020 Faith and Fellowship Book Festival. A local high school invited me to speak to the health class about eating disorders multiple times. Over the next few years, I spoke at a state conference for those in College Student Development, the field in which I had earned my Master of Science degree after college. With each step along the way, my confidence grew. I saw people respond to what I shared. I had done the hard work of healing and now it was time to share that with others and help them. I didn't know what that could look like. I only knew I wanted to be used by God to help others.

In January 2020 my phone rang with an unexpected call from a friend, one whose words hold sway in my life. She had a question for me.

"Have you ever thought about becoming a life coach? It seems that's where you're headed anyway."

"No, I haven't. I'm not sure what that is, but it sounds like snake oil to me."

I spent the next couple of months researching the field. I prayed about it, considering my friend's words. Before long, I found an award-winning and reputable program and earned my certification as a life coach. Later that year I took the advanced training and became a "master certified" life coach.

My speaking opportunities continued to grow. I was a guest on over a hundred podcasts in two years. I continued speaking at state conferences and expanded to speak at national conferences as well as on college campuses. In my speaking and coaching I was hearing a theme. It was familiar to me as I had experienced similar thoughts while I struggled—the whisper of doubt.

"You don't know my story. There's no way I could do that."

"It's too late for me. I've raised my family. Now I just find something to keep me busy."

"Do you think it could really be true for me? Really?"

"I'm too screwed up. There's no hope for me anymore."

I wrestled with similar doubts after my parents passed away. I was Mom's caregiver, and Dad was my biggest cheerleader and loudest supporter. I felt I lost my identity as well as my encourager. Who would cheer me on now? I had to answer the same question I posed to my audiences. Do I believe that I matter?

The "Dare to Believe Movement" was born from these questions. In listening to the stories entrusted to me from my coaching clients and my audiences, I became convinced that until each of us can answer "Do *I* believe that I matter?" in a positive, bedrock way, permanent life change cannot and will not happen. It's not enough for someone else to believe in us. We must answer it for ourselves.

Our stories are full of messages others have told us. Every trauma tells us we don't matter, or that we are "less than." The things we tell ourselves carry even more weight. We can't get away from our thoughts. We believe lies as truth and lose our true north. Before long, we believe in the lie that we don't matter. We've built on a faulty foundation. We must tear it down before it can be rebuilt.

The challenge is how to rebuild. Our thoughts have proven unreliable. We lose trust in ourselves and others, not knowing where to turn. Lies, self-talk, and fear monopolize our thoughts. Until we draw the line in the sand that announces, "It ends now." When someone dares you, they challenge you to do something outside of your comfort zone. They see something in you before you may see it in yourself. Even if you don't yet feel it. That's my challenge for you.

Breaking the Silence

I dare you to believe you matter!

One must dare to stop the cycle, to step out of the negative patterns that have held you back. What does that mean and what does that look like?

First, you must face the fear. Life does not change until you face your fears. Fear wears many faces and whispers a myriad of lies. Those lies keep you captive, and they didn't get there on their own. Neither will they go away on their own. You have tried dealing with it yourself. It hasn't worked. It's time to get help.

Pride gets in the way of accepting help. Quick to help others, it's often difficult to accept help. Pride keeps you in the prison of your mind until you humble yourself and admit you don't have it all figured out. Inviting others into your story lightens the burden and begins to defeat the lie that isolation will protect you. Isolation will kill you.

I dare you to believe that you matter. You may feel you have nothing to offer, or your story has no weight because you're still figuring it out. I'm daring you to believe anyway. Your story has worth. You have worth. And your story can help someone else in theirs. The best part is you may never know! When Simone Biles shared her story in 2018, it gave me permission to tell mine and helped me step from my prison of shame and doubt. She doesn't know. I hope I have an opportunity to tell her personally at some point. That is the power of sharing your story.

So, what does being daring look like? It looks different for each person. Maybe it's calling a counselor or life coach. It could be apologizing for a long-harbored resentment. Perhaps it's breaking free from a bad situation where you are manipulated and gas lit. However, the important thing is to take the step. Step out of your comfort zone. Break the mold. Forge a new path.

Daring is taking positive steps or ending negative things. It's speaking up, asking for help, and taking a risk. It's doing whatever communicates to yourself that you have worth in any given situation.

John 4:50 (NIV) is one of my favorite Bible verses. It simply says, "The man took Jesus at His word and departed." If the Roman soldier sought out Jesus to heal his child, and believed

Breaking the Silence

Jesus was good for His word before the soldier even got home, why can't we take Jesus at His word for what He says about us? The only answer is pride. In one way or another, it comes down to pride.

What is stirring in your heart after reading my story? You are not disqualified. Your story uniquely qualifies you to help others, just as my story has uniquely qualified me to help you right now. My Step Ahead and the Dare to Believe Movement are here to serve you. What is your next step on your journey? I would love to hear your story or what's stirring in you. I can be reached through my website and email below.

You matter, you have worth, and your story can help someone even while you heal. Permanent life change cannot and will not happen until you can answer the question "Do I believe I matter?" with a resounding yes. I believe you matter. Do *you* believe that you matter?

ABOUT THE AUTHOR

Sue Bowles is a survivor-turned-thriver as an award-winning and Amazon best-selling author, speaker, Master Certified Life and Board-Certified Master Mental Health Coach. Having done the hard work of healing from a childhood rape, an eating disorder, other sexual assaults, and twice considering suicide, Sue uses these life-altering events to catalyze new hope for others. Now, as the Chief Instigator behind the Dare to Believe Movement and Founder of My Step Ahead LLC, Sue leads the charge in talking about real things that matter. She gets to the heart of the issue where true breakthroughs and change happen. Through speaking, writing, and coaching, she challenges others who feel stuck and disqualified due to life circumstances to take the next step in their journey, walking with them along the way so they can live boldly in Christ and fulfill their God-given calling.

My Step Ahead is committed to empowering others to share their story while they heal, launching the Dare to Believe Movement in 2022 to challenge thoughts and spur actionable change in lives. The website, www.daretobelievemovement.com offers a variety of resources, including free downloadable articles and worksheets to begin your daring journey, as well as the free PDF booklet, "Dare to Believe! Making Yesterday's Setbacks Tomorrow's Success."

Sue's first book, *This Much I Know ... The Space Between* was published in 2019. She is also a contributing author of *Breaking the Silence: Voices of Survivors Vol 1*. Both books can be purchased through Sue's website at www.suebowles.com.

Sue is a sought-after international podcast guest and national conference speaker. Her favorite part of speaking events is meeting the audience afterward to learn more about their stories. As a life coach, Sue is ready to help you take the next step on your healing journey. Sue is also available to speak to your group, campus, retreat, conference, or organization and can be reached at sue@suebowles.com

For more information on Walking Stick Retreats, go to walkingstickretreats.org.

CHAPTER 3

THE PATH TO PEACE

Michelle Turnbull

    The night was palpable, a tangible darkness that draped over my life like an uninvited cloak. Amidst this shadowed stillness, the echoing beep of machines gave way to a chilling silence—a flatline that marked the end of an era. No more heartbeat. No more breath. No more laughter. No more hugs. No more kisses. No more Mom. The emptiness left in her absence was a vicious void that no amount of time could fill.

    My mother was a warrior in her own right, a seemingly invincible force who had weathered numerous battles with her health. To me, she seemed coated in Teflon; nothing could stick to her, not even the darkest diagnoses. Yet, on that fateful night, as I lay beside her, something was unsettlingly weighing on me. The air was thick with an ominous sense, a silent acknowledgment of something none of us dared to voice. In our final moments together, her spirit seemed to reach for something beyond, connecting with loved ones long passed as she recalled memories from her distant youth. This is typically called the "crossing over" or "transitioning" phase of life.

    We sang gospel hymns together, her voice weak but determined— "This Little Light of Mine," "Jesus Loves Me," "What a Friend We Have in Jesus." These melodies, repeated in the quiet of her room, felt like a gentle farewell, a soothing balm for wounds yet to be fully realized. She spoke to me with an intensity that pierced the growing veil between us, ensuring her love was the last truth I heard from her lips.

    That night, after a restless transition to sleep, I was suddenly awakened—not by a sound, but by a profound sense of finality. A dreamlike bell tolled, followed by a burst of white light, urging me downstairs. It was there I faced the irrevocable truth: she had departed. No more warmth of her presence, no goodbye, just a piercing, indescribable pain. This time, her body had surrendered to a fight it could no longer endure.

Breaking the Silence

In her last days, our home had transformed into a sanctuary filled with the presence of those she had touched—friends old and new, sorority sisters of Alpha Kappa Alpha, members of the Freshwater Yankees Virgin Islands Association, and countless others who had been graced by her spirit. Aunt Lea, her steadfast sister, had taken on the mantle of caregiver, pouring out love and strength as my mother's life quietly dimmed.

After her passing, the bustling energy of visitors evaporated as quickly as it had gathered. Silence reclaimed the space, leaving me alone with the echoes of her last days and the songs we shared. The absence of her laughter and the cessation of our shared hymns marked the beginning of a solitary journey—a journey of carrying her legacy and the pain of her loss.

The funeral was a testament to her silent influence—a crowded gathering of lives she had touched, hearts she had warmed. She may not have been a celebrity in the world's eyes, but to those who knew her, she was an earthly angel, a bearer of light and love. People stood, filling every available space, united in mourning and celebration of a life genuinely lived.

As I stood there, amidst the crowd, I felt both connected to and utterly detached from the world around me. The weight of her absence was a constant companion. I began journaling, and these thoughts, the recounting of my journey, became my therapy. It was here, in the written word and the memories etched on each page, that I sought to find my path through the labyrinth of grief, guided by the light of her enduring love.

Grief, like a silent thief, had stolen the vibrancy from my life, leaving behind a dense fog of depression that settled around me, thick and isolating. This suffocating mist blurred the boundaries of time, rendering days indistinguishable from each other and weeks melded into a continuous loop of despair. In this obscured reality, the warmth of social gatherings, once a source of comfort and joy, became daunting tasks. Each invitation was a reminder of the effort required to merely exist among others, an effort that seemed increasingly Herculean.

Friends who once relished in my laughter and lightness now found themselves confronting a shell of my former self. I was

Breaking the Silence

engulfed by loss, so deeply submerged in sorrow that reaching out or letting others in felt like navigating an insurmountable barrier. Consequently, my social life dwindled, not just in the frequency of engagements, but in the very willingness to partake in what life still had to offer. The retreat was not a choice but a compulsion, driven by the overwhelming weight of memories and the palpable absence of hope.

In this altered state of being, hope was no longer a beacon guiding me forward but a flickering flame, easily smothered by the relentless winds of despair. The future, which once appeared as a vibrant tapestry of endless possibilities, now loomed before me as an intimidating blank page. The very thought of attempting to add color to it was exhausting. Every day served as a stark reminder of the losses I had endured—the absence of those who had shaped my very being—and with each reminder, the vibrancy of life faded further into the monotonous grays of my grief.

Amidst this landscape of sorrow, the seductive escape offered by alcohol and drugs began to weave its way into my existence. Luckily, it never escalated to hard drugs, but it was an addictive factor, nonetheless. These substances presented a temporary reprieve, a way to dull the acute edges of my pain. Nights became a ritual of numbness, where the bottom of a bottle or the momentary high felt like a needed respite from the relentless pain and isolation. However, each morning brought back the stark reality, unaltered and often magnified by the aftereffects of my choices.

The repercussions of my increasing dependency were profound. Relationships that had once been sources of strength and stability began to crumble under the strain of my seclusion, and the erratic behaviors fueled by my attempts to escape reality. The few connections that remained were strained, marred by misunderstandings and the mutual pain of seeing what I had become.

Suicidal ideations began to surface, insidious thoughts that whispered of a more permanent solution to the unbearable pain. These thoughts were both terrifying and seductive, offering an end to the relentless grief that had become my constant companion.

Breaking the Silence

The battle with these dark contemplations became yet another secret struggle, one that I fought in the silent hours of the night, often feeling alone in a seemingly endless fight.

As I navigated this treacherous terrain, the necessity for transformation became increasingly clear. The shadows of yesterday were not just remnants to be mourned but profound challenges to be met head-on. These painful reflections were crucial, for they highlighted both the depth of my despair and the potential paths forward. Through therapy, introspection, and the tentative rekindling of neglected relationships, I began to acknowledge the need for healing—not just for the losses of my beloved parents but for the person I had become in the wake of their departure.

Healing was neither quick nor linear. It required the dismantling of the very foundations of my grief and the careful construction of a new identity—one that could both honor the past and embrace the future. Support groups, counseling, and the slow reintegration into social settings played pivotal roles in this arduous journey. Each step forward was a testament to the resilience of the human spirit, a spirit that, despite everything, refused to be extinguished.

In this painstaking process, I found new ways to connect with the memories of my parents without being anchored by the pain associated with their absence. I learned to carry the love and lessons they imparted not as weights but as guiding lights. Gradually, the blank pages of the future began to fill with sparks of hope and possibilities, painted not in spite of the grief but because of the growth it had precipitated.

As the echoes of my past life reverberated around me, my journey through the shadows of yesterday towards the light of tomorrow continued. With each step, I was not leaving my past behind but transforming it into a strength that propelled me forward, into a future where the memories of lost loved ones illuminated the path ahead, guiding me through the uncharted territory of a life rebuilt on the foundation of resilience and renewed hope.

Breaking the Silence

The world had become a series of before and afters: before my mother passed, after she left, and then, the world after my stepdad joined her. His passing, while gut-wrenching, carried with it a different kind of legacy—a promise made not through words but through understanding and shared silences. He knew the depths of my struggle with my mother's death better than anyone. He wasn't just my stepdad; he was the anchor in the stormy seas of my grief. When he left, it wasn't just a loss; it was a call to action. A final nudge to step out of the shadows and into the light.

As the executor of his estate, I suddenly found myself in a role that was about as comfortable as a cactus in a balloon factory. Trust me, navigating a family that suddenly regarded me with the suspicion reserved for outsiders in a tight-knit village was no walk in the park. He had warned me, though. "Keep your eyes open, and your heart guarded," my stepdad advised, his words now a constant echo in my head. In the snake pit of greed and familial tension, his belief in me was the shield I carried.

Writing this is no easy task; it's like trying to dance ballet on a tightrope—painfully beautiful and terrifying. But tell it I must. As I ventured into the present, a newfound understanding that healing required action, not just contemplation, took root. I couldn't run away from the places steeped in pain; I needed to transform them. My home, once a mausoleum of memories, needed a new coat of paint—figuratively and literally.

Every corner of my house, every cobblestone on my street whispered of past pains and echoed laughter long silenced. I began to paint over these memories, not to erase them but to blend them into a new scene. If I couldn't immediately find happiness outside, I decided to cultivate it right where I was. I started with turning the room where I had spent countless hours ruminating into a bright studio filled with paints, brushes, and canvases. Here, the only blues allowed were those squeezed from a tube onto a palette.

Conquering my fear of flying was another unexpected chapter in my journey. Who knew that the girl who once got woozy at the sight of an airplane safety demonstration would one day look out of a plane window without hyperventilating? But there I was, soaring above the clouds, finding my peace in the

Breaking the Silence

skies. Each trip became a chapter of its own in the textbook of my life. From the bustling streets of Chicago and Atlanta to the serene views of Niagara Falls, each location held lessons in resilience and pieces of a new me waiting to be discovered.

These travels were my bridge over troubled waters. I learned to navigate through Chicago's architectural marvels, soaked up the vibrant culture in Atlanta, and marveled at the breathtaking rush of Niagara Falls. I reveled in the tropical beauty of Punta Cana, felt the rhythmic pulse of Carnival in St. Thomas, and rediscovered serenity and my familial connection in the British Virgin Islands. Each destination was a stroke on the canvas of my new reality, splashing my world with colors I never knew I needed.

And oh, the people I met! Each one added a thread to the tapestry of my evolving life. Falling in love? I fell in love with love again. Well, it happened more times than I'd care to admit. Not just with people, but with places, with moments. There were kindred spirits everywhere, each encounter enriching my journey, teaching me about the boundless capacities of the human heart. And to have complete strangers believe in my capabilities more than me is something that doesn't carry words.

Each return home to St. Thomas was a return to my workshop of self—my sanctuary where every new experience was molded into a stepping stone. The more I traveled, the more the essence of each place seeped into my being, transforming not just my inner landscape but also my physical one. My home now boasted a collection of mementos: pictures of Chicago's skyline, a peach from Georgia, and shells from the shores of the Dominican Republic.

Indeed, this journey was about finding happiness not just in the places I visited but in the recesses of my own soul. It was about understanding that while grief had once threatened to define my life, the narrative was mine to rewrite. Humor became my unexpected companion, lighting my steps and reminding me that life, despite its occasional thorns, was meant to be embraced fully—sometimes with a laugh, even if it was through tears.

As I continue to chart my course through the present, the promise I made to my stepdad remains a guiding star. With each

Breaking the Silence

day, I strive not just to live but to thrive, honoring his memory and my journey with every breath, every stroke of paint, every flight that takes me to new heights. This story of transformation is far from over, but oh, what a plot twist life has offered.

Where I stand today is a testament to the journey I've endured—a path marked by immense pain, profound loss, and, most importantly, incredible growth. I am a work in progress, constantly evolving, learning, and adapting. Life, as I've come to understand, is not about avoiding problems or escaping challenges. It's about facing them head-on, learning to navigate through them, and using each experience to forge a stronger self.

This narrative I've crafted is not just a recounting of past sorrows and triumphs; it is an ode to life, a celebration of the resilience I've managed to harness in the face of adversity. My journey has been about building from the ground up, creating a life that resonates with the essence of who I am and who I aspire to be.

The tools of my transformation have been varied and vital. Retreats have become my sanctuaries, places where I can disconnect from the world's noise and listen intently to the whispers of my own soul. These retreats have not just been escapes but recalibrations, opportunities to realign with my goals and re-energize my spirit.

Building relationships has been another cornerstone of my growth. Learning to let people in was not an overnight change but a deliberate practice. Each new relationship challenged the walls I had built around my heart, coaxing me into a world where vulnerability is not a liability but a strength. Through these connections, I've constructed a robust framework for success—one anchored in genuine interactions and mutual support.

Networking has expanded my horizons, connecting me with individuals whose insights and experiences have enriched my understanding and appreciation of the world. Each connection has been a thread in the larger tapestry of my life, revealing patterns and possibilities I had never imagined.

Self-therapy emerged as a critical tool when traditional therapy didn't meet my needs. It was through self-reflection and dedicated personal work that I learned the most about myself—my triggers, my boundaries, and my capacities for change. This practice of self-dialogue and introspection became my steady companion, guiding me through moments of doubt and reaffirming my belief in my potential.

Celebrating my victories, big and small, has been crucial. Each accomplishment, whether a completed project or a personal breakthrough, is a testament to my perseverance and tenacity. These celebrations are reminders of my capabilities, reinforcing the message to myself and the world: I am capable, I am resilient, and I am worthy of every success.

Looking forward, I understand that healing is not a linear journey or a permanent state. It is a continuous process, susceptible to setbacks and triggers that can momentarily send me spiraling back to darker times. However, I remind myself daily of the distance I've traveled, the barriers I've overcome. The resilience I've cultivated is not just about bouncing back but also about springing forward.

The road ahead is laden with promise and potential. As I continue this voyage, I do so with a spirit of determination and optimism. I know that the best is yet to come, not as a hope but as a reality I'm actively constructing. Each step forward is a deliberate move towards a future where I am not just surviving but thriving.

In embracing my role as a "boss," I've taken control of my narrative. I refuse to let anyone diminish my achievements or dictate my path. I stand firm in my resolve, powered by the knowledge that I possess the tools, the courage, and the support network to face whatever comes my way.

This journey is about more than just personal success; it's about setting a precedent for resilience and empowerment. It's about showing others that, despite the depths of despair we may face, each of us has an inner strength waiting to be unleashed. It's about proving that even when the world seems against us, we have the power to rewrite the script, to turn our trials into triumphs.

As I chart my course forward, I do so with an eye towards not just improving myself but also impacting those around me. My story is one of countless others, each echoing the universal truths of human endurance and the transformative power of hope.

    This is not just a farewell to past pains but a heralding of future successes. It is a declaration of ongoing transformation, a continuous embrace of life's complexities. As I move forward, I am reminded of the simple yet profound truth: every day is a step towards becoming the person I am meant to be. This is my unyielding commitment to progress—to live fully, love deeply, and lead boldly, with every sunrise promising not just a new day but a new opportunity for growth and joy. This is where I am heading, not just navigating life but celebrating it, every step of the way.

ABOUT THE AUTHOR

    At the heart of every transformative journey lies a storyteller, weaving experiences of resilience and renewal into narratives that reach out and resonate with others. The author of this powerful story is a vibrant 45-year-old Caribbean-American woman whose life echoes the rich tapestry of cultures and experiences she has navigated. A former educator, her journey into writing is not merely a career shift but a passionate endeavor to share her truths with an audience that seeks both solace and inspiration in the pages of a deeply personal yet universally relevant story.

    Born and raised in a culture known for its warmth, rhythm, and color, she brings the same vibrancy and intensity to her writing. Her Caribbean heritage of St. Thomas, Virgin Islands, steeped in a history of overcoming, plays a foundational role in her narrative, shaping her voice and infusing her stories with a unique perspective that is both enlightening and empowering.

    Her professional background as an educator for over three decades has equipped her with profound insights into the human spirit's resilience. In the classroom, she witnessed firsthand the struggles and triumphs of young minds, an experience that has deeply influenced her writing. Her transition from educator to author was driven by a desire to reach a broader audience, to teach beyond the confines of the traditional classroom, and to engage with readers in a dialogue about life's deepest challenges and greatest triumphs.

This author writes not only to tell her story but to connect with others who have faced their own battles with grief, loss, and personal transformation. Her narrative is a beacon for those navigating the tumultuous waters of change, providing both a compass and a comfort through her honest and heartfelt prose. She crafts her chapter with a blend of raw emotion and refined artistry, making her readers feel deeply seen and profoundly understood.

Her life's work is a testament to her belief in the power of storytelling as therapy, as a means of healing, and as a way to forge connections across diverse experiences. Through her writing, she aims to empower her readers, offering them not just a story, but a shared experience of overcoming and evolving.

Has Michelle's story and experiences resonated with you? We invite you to share your own journey and how you've navigated your challenges. Connect with Michelle on the following social media platforms. Let's build a community of support and resilience together! Stay tuned for other ways to engage with the community and transform your life.

Facebook: Michelle Turnbull
https://www.facebook.com/michelle.turnbull.5680/
Instagram: Chellyt340 https://www.instagram.com/chellyt340/
LinkedIn: Michelle Turnbull
www.linkedin.com/in/turnbullcoaching

CHAPTER 4

NAVIGATING GRIEF:

A JOURNEY OF LOSS, RELISIENCE, AND REDISCOVERY

Tami Imlay

Losing Myself

Ten minutes from home, my mind was on "the window." You know what I'm talking about. This incredibly short window between getting the two toddlers home, fed, and in bed for nap time. You miss the window, and it is a rough night. I mistakenly thought that bedtime would be a breeze if toddlers missed naps, and I had been burned before, so I did not miss the window. I live for nap time. I have some time to myself for a short forty-five to ninety minutes with both kids tucked into their beds. Taking care of two extremely active toddlers was exhausting and exhilarating, and I needed the nap time.

I had already made the plans. The fruit was cut, chicken nuggets were ready to go in the oven, and sippy cups were filled with "juice" (95 percent water and 5 percent lemonade). I knew spending the morning over an hour away at a bounce house center for a birthday party was going to wipe the kids out, and they would be primed for nap time. I was seeing the finish line, I had successfully engaged the kids for the last fifty minutes of the drive, keeping them awake. The plan was working, and I saw freedom.

I wasn't a single mom, but I was a solo mom. My husband, an Air Force fighter pilot, was often gone, and my relief was when the kids were sleeping. I rounded the corner of the neighborhood. Success! The kids' heads were starting to bounce, but they were both still awake. The garage door went up, so I drove in and came to a stop. Instantly, the dog started barking while we were singing the lunchtime song. I walked in loaded down with bags, empty sippy cups, diapers, and trash. I was in the window.

Kids were heading to the table and already starting to show signs that I might have missed the window. I stayed the course. Then there was a knock at the door.

Breaking the Silence

My thoughts raced. "Did I grab an extra sippy cup?" All my friends were with me at the party, so it was odd that they would stop by unannounced. I thought, "Who does this anymore ... knocking on the door and stopping by without a phone call or text? No one! If this is the vacuum guy and he makes me miss the window, so help me ..." I went to the door, and three men in service dress were standing there.

My mind went blank. Why are they here? What do they want? What do they need? Questions flew in my mind as panic set in.

"Mrs. Imlay, can we come in?"

"Umm, sure. I guess. What is this about?" I don't know why, at this time, I didn't know what was about to come out of their mouths. I have seen a thousand movies with this moment. I have been a part of this detail before, preparing three leaders to go to an unsuspecting family and knock on the door. But my brain was protecting me. I remember thinking, "Oh, they have something good to tell me." The look on their faces said it wasn't anything good.

"Mrs. Imlay, there has been an accident."

Still, my brain was racing and my body collapsed. Isaac and Lyndis came over, tapping on my shoulder, "Mommy, I'm hungry," "Mommy, who are these people?" "Mommy, why are you crying? Are you sad?" I didn't realize I was crying; I had no idea what was happening. "Mommy ... Mommy ... Mommy ..." The kids kept talking as the men continued.

"Mrs. Imlay, there has been an accident. Your husband didn't survive."

Wait, what? He was an amazing pilot. My mind was starting to wake up and consider the cruel joke—aren't they supposed to notify us before they go through an "exercise protocol?" Dee had won an Air Force-wide award just years before called The Golden Hands Award for flying through an emergency situation and handling it with valor.

They had this wrong. This had to be wrong. I had just talked to Dee not more than twelve hours ago. He had only been deployed for two weeks! TWO WEEKS! He doesn't even know his way around the base yet. There is no way.

"Ma'am, is there someone you need to call?"

I remember feeling like I was responding unjustly rude: "Yes, I need to call someone!" My mind was still in shock and still didn't feel real. I told myself, "Don't be rude, Tami. They are here, and they don't want to be either." My mind was still not comprehending what was happening. All I wanted to do was get the kids in bed. I wanted a few moments to myself. How was I blindsided with my world collapsing?

I remember someone handing me the diaper bag, where my phone was. I dug through and called my friend Krista, I was just with her. She wouldn't even be home yet. I remember calling her, saying, "Get here now," and hanging up. I then called my dad. "Dad, Dee's dead. I need you."

"I'll fly out as soon as I can."

Living in Idaho, I didn't have family local. I didn't have family by blood, but over the next few weeks, I realized that I had something much stronger than blood. I had a brotherhood around me, a community supporting me and living for me.

I was on the floor, and Krista swooped in, not knowing what to expect, but went straight to work getting the kids fed and taken care of. At that moment, I could feel a weight on my shoulder, though nothing was there. I could hear the voice that could only be from God whispering, "Tami, this is going to be hard, but you aren't alone. This will be used for good." I remember being comforted by it and embracing this was not about me, but knowing this was my life now. I didn't even know what that meant.

I discovered that a plane crash and ejection had occurred, and Dee didn't survive. I didn't get details because the accident was under investigation, and they only gave me the little they could. I knew they were holding back. It didn't matter, my body couldn't handle it anyway.

Within seventy-two hours of hearing the death, I was forced to make decisions I never knew I would. The Air Force flew my family, Dee's family, and some of the squadron members to

Breaking the Silence

Dover, Delaware, to receive Dee and make plans. I'm thankful I was assigned someone who supported and protected me. His call sign was "Money" and I learned that he specifically asked for the assignment. He was one of Dee's mentors and felt compelled to step in. He walked me through hours of paperwork and would step in when I was getting overwhelmed. He was there to take care of all the logistics so I could focus on one thing at a time. I needed him.

The squadron didn't stop there. Dee's friends "Rouge" and "Scar" each cared for one of the kids. I don't remember changing a diaper or feeding the kids in that first week. I knew they were taken care of. It was hard enough to just breathe.

The next few weeks were a blurry whirlwind. The funeral plans were made. I chose a burial site. I remember how food showed up, and dishes ended up washed. I remember how the kids had someone come and play with them, and I would walk. For weeks, someone came every day to walk with me. Sometimes, we would talk, other times, silence. No matter what, someone was there. I didn't realize then how much I needed someone. All I remember was how grateful I was that I wasn't alone. I didn't have to think, the squadron took care of it all.

Weeks turned into months, and the grief set in and got deeper. Still not understanding life, survival mode kicked in. My brain started to play the events over and over. The final thought was always, "I lost my husband, my best friend, my high school sweetheart, the father to my kids. How? Why?"

I started trying to do "normal" things like cooking and cleaning, but still I depended on the people around me. I knew people watched me. They were always worried about upsetting me. They were afraid to say the wrong things. The truth was there were no "right things" to say. I had some people distance themselves from me, and I don't blame them. I became a reminder of what could happen. The squadron was still deployed and all the spouses prayed their husbands would come home.

Deep sorrow became a part of my soul. I had Isaac and Lyndis, and at four and two, they had no idea what was happening. One day, Lyndis grabbed my hand, pulled me to the computer, and scolded me, "Call Daddy NOW!" she demanded. We were used to talking to him over Skype. This was the longest she had gone without seeing or talking to him, and she had no idea how her life had changed at two years old. I resolved that day that I would live for them.

A year later, we moved to California to be closer to Dee's parents. I wanted them to be a part of their grandkids' lives. Leaving Idaho as a family of three was so hard, but it was necessary. Most of my close friends were about to be reassigned to different bases, and I knew it was time to make a change.

There was no "normal" at that point. It was survival, caring for the kids, and loving them. A year passed. I managed the different areas of my life. I managed my energy and became less social. I managed my life and took care of the kids, but I wasn't truly living. It was too hard.

Understanding the Loss

In the fall of 2013, about eighteen months after the accident, I started to recognize the thick grief fog that was surrounding me. It wasn't starting to dissipate, but I became aware of it. I started to become aware of the safety armor I had layered on me and the kids. This was the point that I looked at my life. I realized that not only did I lose my love, my partner, and my culture (I had been born on an Air Force base ... the Air Force was always a part of me), but I realized I lost *myself*. I lost the ability to dream and create goals, I lost the essence of who I was. And I became okay with it.

I wasn't ready to start shedding the armor of protection I crafted. I still needed it. I didn't realize the barriers and boundaries I had put up around me for survival. I don't regret the armor, but I more and more realize how it held me back. It was limiting my life to survival and I wasn't getting to experience the full range of emotions that are needed for truly living life. I needed the safeguard, I wanted it, it was necessary ... until now.

I felt like I was starting to wake up. Reality was setting in, and I could see that I was at a crossroads. I was living but not loving life. I needed a change. I needed to create a new way of being. It was time to embrace the future and boldly walk into it.

Being in the "widow club," I had a first-row seat to my future if I allowed the deep sorrow of grief to lead my decisions. I could see the different outcomes possible. When it came down to it, I could see three clear options.

Option one: Succumb to grief. Allow grief and loss to be the central theme of your life and choose daily activities that surround grief. Put your loved one as the reason for all decisions and live like your life died when they died. This harsh reality is one that many of my friends chose. The need for their "legacy" to be kept and memories that needed to remain alive meant that they died to themselves. The full weight of grief surrounds you and controls you. This option is centered around fear and the past. I knew this wasn't what I wanted for myself or my kids.

Option two: Rush grief. Check the boxes, read the books, and in the famous words of Elsa, from the movie *Frozen*, "Conceal, don't feel." Move past grief and convince yourself that "it is what it is." You embrace comments like "can't change the past" and "can't get it back." You decide to put the past behind you and only look forward.

At first, this might seem like an efficient way to get through grief. Do the therapy, attend the groups, get to a point of understanding, and push forward. The problem with this option is you miss the healing part of the grief process. You miss the gifts of grief that are meant for you. You are so afraid to feel that barriers are put up to limit your daily emotions. The weight of the world is upon you. Constantly avoiding reminders and changing the subject. The intention is to limit the deep, dark, hard emotions, but the thing is, you can only feel the joy at the same depth as the sorrow.

When you put up barriers around negative feelings, you are also allowing the positive emotions to be limited. This option enables you to numb your feelings. All of them. I knew this wasn't what I wanted for my kids. At first glance, I thought that it would be okay to numb out, at least the crying would stop. But so does the laughter.

Breaking the Silence

Option three: Live grief. Walk through your journey of grief and learn to partner with it instead of being controlled by it or avoiding it. This path, by far, is the hardest. You feel every emotion as it comes. One day, you are crying, and the next, you are laughing. Eventually, it becomes moment-to-moment rather than day-to-day. You experience the full range of emotions and are able to laugh and experience the full weight of joy. Your life becomes your own. You get to find yourself in your story and live a full life. The legacy you want to leave is about honor and growth rather than holding on to a life that no longer exists.

You learn your strengths and weaknesses. You learn why you grieve the way you do, and the surprising thing about this ... as you learn about your grief, you, for the first time possibly ever, learn about your joy. This is what I wanted for myself and for my kids.

Finding Myself

I wasn't just going through grief myself; I was raising grieving kids who were learning about the world through the eyes of grief. They never got to experience life without grief. They never had a clear view of the crystal ball or through the rose-colored glasses. I knew their lives would be forever tainted by the trauma and fears of grief if I didn't do something now. I knew that if I didn't choose option three, they would never know to choose it for themselves.

I made the choice not to allow grief to define my life. I knew it wasn't enough to help them through grief. If I didn't put on my oxygen mask first and do the hard work of healing, they would never learn to do it for themselves either. I wanted to model a beautiful life, not just fabricate one or put on a play for the world. I defined what I wanted to be and who I wanted to be as a mom, friend, and woman. I made a decision that day. I would stop being led by grief, allowing the ebb and flow of feelings to dictate my actions or decisions. Feelings have never been a good leader. I would intentionally choose *my* path, *my* options, and I decided I was going on a quest to heal. A quest to live. A quest to love. And it started with me.

Breaking the Silence

The Quest

I wanted to know the how and why. I wanted to know what happened to our brains and our bodies when we grieved. I wasn't satisfied with the books I read, the therapy I went to, or the superficial journaling I attempted. I wanted real answers. I wanted to stop checking the boxes and appear to be healing. I wanted to be healed ... NOW!

After a terrible grief therapy experience, I decided that I would go back to school to be a therapist. My friends encouraged me and agreed that this was the right path. This was what I was meant to do. My first step was to enroll in school. I went back for my second master's program, but this time, it was for me and not for a job. I went to school for a master's in the Science of Marriage, Family, and Child Therapy, with an emphasis on grief.

The Body

I learned about how our bodies hold our grief and emotions deep in our veins. I learned that by experiencing these emotions of grief and giving it a voice in our lives, we are releasing its hold. Grief has to get out one way or another. If you don't willingly release the deep emotions, they come out in somatic ways (hair loss, weight gain or loss, back pain, lumps, cancer). Grief is not only relentless on our hearts, it's cruel to our bodies as well.

I experienced the common weight gain and loss that came with grief, but I wasn't expecting the other somatic experiences. Within weeks of my husband's death, I had my menstrual cycle every other week for about six months. In order to "stop it," I was put on medication that stopped the bleeding but also increased my weight by twenty pounds.

I was told not to eat so much to combat the weight gain. What they didn't know was, I wasn't eating. I had a bowl of Cheerios and then the scraps from my kids' plates—a leftover chicken nugget or a few carrots. There is no "normal" reaction in the midst of grief. Your body does what it wants to do. Your body cries out as much as your heart does.

Breaking the Silence

The Mind

I discovered the science of how grief changed our brains. I loved art, but the idea of being creative became foreign. Six ladies at my house created elaborate and unique greeting cards just days before the accident. Creativity was always a way of expressing my deepest desires and the thought of picking up a paintbrush or pair of scissors hurt as my mind went to "What's the point?" I longed for meaning in anything ordinary. My world died. My creativity and expected thought patterns died as well. The things that made sense before no longer applied to my grieving brain.

Our brains and body adapt to survival. The physical makeup of our being changes as much as our soul does. Grief is a visceral experience that can't be explained until you become intimate with it. Each person has a unique experience. As I studied, I saw patterns and started to become acquainted with why I had the reactions I did versus what other widows had experienced. It became clear how our brains were wired for survival, and though all the basic needs were the same, our journeys were not.

The Gifts of Grief – Loving Myself

Making the decision to find myself through the grief proved to be one of the most rewarding experiences I had ever gone through. It was one of the most grueling and heartbreaking paths as well. I do not regret one moment, one tear, one determined and exhausting decision. As I found myself, I learned to love myself. As the bruises and wounds turned to scars, I began growing, healing, and learning to dream again. I became a deeper, more compassionate person. I learned to open my heart to love life. I grew stronger and took charge of my decisions. I embraced the trials as they came, knowing I could find a way through. I began to thrive, and life became more vibrant and joyful than ever; I knew this was just the beginning.

As I grew stronger and shed the layers of armor, I remembered the calm whisper as I sat on the floor, hearing how my world had come crashing down: "This will be used for good." New hope flooded through my veins like a dam being released and water rushing into the river. I discovered strength in vulnerability and faith in a God of grace like I had never known. My journey of grief transformed into a journey of purpose.

My life had new meaning, and the crazy part was that I realized it was always there. I just hadn't taken the time to embody it. The gifts that I learned through deep grief became the gifts that propelled my calling.

ABOUT THE AUTHOR

Tami Imlay lives on a small farm in Oklahoma, where she finds peace and inspiration surrounded by nature and family. A military BRAT and Air Force veteran, Tami carries the spirit of adventure in her heart, always ready for the next journey. Her impressive academic credentials include an MBA and a Master of Science in Marriage, Family, and Child Therapy.

After enduring a life-altering tragedy, Tami transformed her pain into purpose, starting her own business to help others do the same. She is the host of the inspiring podcast *The Full Weight of Joy*, where she shares stories of resilience and growth, reaching listeners around the world. As an International Women's Achievement Coach, Tami holds multiple master certifications in coaching, enriching her expertise in science, behavioral health, and strategy. She has the privilege of speaking, writing, and coaching women all over the world.

Tami's mission is to guide women out of life's numbness and into a vibrant existence filled with purpose. She empowers her clients to discover their deepest desires, whether it's starting a legacy-building business or uncovering their true selves. Through her compassionate coaching, Tami helps women step boldly into the life they were meant to live.

Her journey is a testament to the strength found in vulnerability and the power of faith. By serving others, Tami has experienced profound healing and now dedicates her life to helping others find their own paths to joy and fulfillment.

To connect with Tami, check out *The Full Weight of Joy* at your favorite place to listen to podcasts and check out http://www.tamimariecoaching.com/breakingthesilence.

CHAPTER 5

THE JOURNEY WITHIN THE JOURNEY BEGINS

Trent Brock

    This is a unique chapter as it is a continuation from Volume One. If you did not get a chance to read it, the next few paragraphs are a summary to get us up to speed.

    I am originally from Louisiana, graduated with an MBA and IT degree from Louisiana Tech University. I traveled around the U.S. and worldwide installing large-scale software systems for big corporations. I ended up in stunningly beautiful New Zealand. After living there for four years, I stumbled upon an opportunity to start a kettle corn business with an American guy that came into my boxing gym. He was a boxing manager and had traveled to New Zealand with a few of his boxers to prepare for matches. In the States he had a side business selling outdoor craft market kettle corn and wondered if it would work in New Zealand. After researching, I thought it would be a winner! Fourteen years in business, we became the number two popcorn manufacturer in New Zealand with fifteen staff, four popcorn lines, and more popcorn products than I could keep track of.

    In the spring of 2019, I started limping around "Popcorn Heaven" (my nickname for the popcorn factory) and was diagnosed with aggressive hip bone cancer. The surgery to remove the cancer was successful but left me with a chronic infection and the physical challenge of my left leg being four inches shorter than the right. Doctors told me that I would never walk again and would be on crutches or a wheelchair the rest of my life. On my next scan I was diagnosed with lung and then pancreatic cancer. I had a less than 5 percent chance of survival). The lung surgery was successful, but there was not anything the doctors would do with the pancreatic cancer. Five surgeons told me I was done for and gave me a year to live. In the spring of 2021, I returned to Northwest Arkansas to be with my family, but I just could not give up on life. We did radiation on the pancreatic tumor that had grown to the size of a softball in seven months, and thank God, we got it. We also cured a two-year chronic infection in my hip to give me a very remote chance at a hip implant with a hopeful opportunity to walk again.

Here is Chapter Two of my story.

After talking with the Mayo Clinic, my parents and I decided to go in person, instead of a telehealth appointment. This was the best option to determine if a hip implant was a feasible possibility. I was still not in shape for flying so a road trip was the default. It was a ten-hour drive one way. You cannot image how sore and painful it was sitting in the car with literally half of your pelvis missing and no butt cheek on the left side.

We were there for several days having various tests conducted, as well as scans and blood work. I had been going to physical therapy, yoga. and lifting weights for months to prepare. The leg had shriveled up like a toothpick after dragging it around for two years with the chronic infection. I would not have been able to live with myself if I would have been the one to blame for not having a life-changing surgery because my leg was not in good enough physical shape.

I passed all the physical tests. I could tell that the Mayo Clinic orthopedic was very surprised at the strength of my left leg. My University of Arkansas Medical System orthopedic advisor told me that I was part of the less than 5 percent that did not have my leg amputated from the type of hip surgery (hemipelvectomy), and of *that* 5 percent, I was in the top 5 percent of the most functional leg he had ever seen. All that hard work and not giving up put me in the right position to have a chance at a hip implant surgery.

The Mayo Clinic orthopedic and I had a good connection at our face-to-face appointment. He consulted with his other colleagues as this was a multi-disciplinary surgery involving four specialists—a plastic surgeon and proctologist for the surgical hernia repair caused from a hip surgery in N.Z., an orthopedic spine specialist and my orthopedic knee/hip specialist, who would be the head facilitating surgeon for the hip implant.

Breaking the Silence

At the end of the appointment, he said, "I think it is possible, but not sure about all four inches." I said, "I'm an all-or-nothing guy. We need a four-inch plan, or I'm not keen."

With some reservation he replied, "Okay, give me some time, and I will come back to you."

After several weeks, he came back with a three-phase plan that lasted over a year. They could do the hip implant and give me two-three inches. After some time, my blood vessels and nerves shrank and will not go back to their original length. If they stretched them too much, it would paralyze the nerves. Then a bone-lengthening procedure was needed to make up the difference to get to four inches. That entailed cutting the femur leg bone in half right above the knee. A rachet system would be inserted into the leg with some keys on each side. For a month or two, I would turn the keys to help the bone grow about a millimeter each day.

The first phase was a temporary hip implant to remove all the scar tissue, repair the surgical hernia, make a nice space for the permanent titanium implant, and ensure there was absolutely no infection.

A botched hip surgery in New Zealand caused a surgical hernia where my guts had literally fallen into my empty hip area. During surgery at Mayo, the doctors could not get all my guts back inside my abdomen from the hip incision, so they had to make an unplanned incision through my midsection. I was told afterwards that my intestines were sitting outside of me on a table for about five hours while they worked on the hip. Once the hip work was finished, they closed that incision and pushed my intestines back inside and sewed up the midsection. This six-hour surgery ended up being twelve long hours. When I woke up, I had been filleted halfway open in the hip area in a t-shaped incision from the front pubic area all the way to the spine and halfway down the side of my thigh. Then there was a bonus of the seven-inch incision from my belly button to my lower pubic region.

I knew the feeling and pain from the hip from eight previous hip surgeries. This midsection incision was a next level painful experience. I did not think that anything could have been as painful as basically cutting my leg off and sewing it back on with a chronic infection the size of a cantaloupe, but I was way wrong.

The midsection incision greatly affected my core. Every single movement felt like I was literally falling on a sword. On a scale of one to ten, it was a twelve. You must move; it is just not an option to lay there like a mummy. You must eat, move for the nurse/doctor, try to go the bathroom, and simply re-adjust. Breathing too deep, sneezing, coughing, burping, passing gas or trying to go to the bathroom ... all hurt! Plus, I took opiates that made me constipated so I dealt with that as well (Oh joy.)

To add to this, the pain management drugs used in the U.S. are different than what worked in N.Z. due to laws and regulations, so we were in a "discovery" phase. I went back and forth with the pain team for about four days trying everything they requested. I was having major physical and mental side effects, and the pain meds were barely working. I was so frustrated. They would always come in as a team of four or five while I was laying there in agony, making me feel very outnumbered.

One of the pain management doctors even commented that watching me in a constant state of scratching is making her itchy! Good heavens. I was scratching myself to the point of bleeding. Then came the suicidal thoughts. I was trying to plan a way that I could go in the bathroom and end it all, but I could not even get out of bed! My emotions were all over the place, and my patience was gone. I had a confrontation with basically everyone that came in my room. My mom, God love her, would just put her head in her hands. I felt terrible for her. I can't believe she stayed in the room with me during those confrontations. Absolutely no doubt, I would not have made it through everything without my parents.

The mental was worse than the physical, and I had to somehow regain control of the situation. I decided to stop taking all the pain meds. The meds were causing more harm than help. I did not know what to do but one thing: start over with a clean slate. I refused everything for twenty-four hours for a full reset. I did not even take ibuprofen. Let me clarify that I only refused pain meds, not other meds that would compromise my health. I do not recommend medication refusal as a normal option, but I did not

Breaking the Silence

know what else to do. The doctors did not believe it, but then they knew I was serious. My local orthopedic from Bentonville, Arkansas was checking on me. I just so happened to be on the phone with him when one of the pain management doctors came in. We all three had an open, candid conversation that also helped facilitate a change in the pain medication direction.

    We all finally got on the same page. To sum it up, I was on a constant ketamine drip (level two, which was the highest level), fentanyl pain pump that I controlled with a button, scheduled IV pain med injections, and oral pain meds. After two-three days, I was in a great mental state while the pain subsided. I got on my feet and walked about a hundred yards on the second day. They released me two days later.

    Recovery was painful, but nothing I had not dealt with before. I spent most of my time lying in bed working on my laptop for Kettle Korn or sitting in Dad's big lazy boy chair. After about five weeks, my folks went to the movie one Friday afternoon. Our dog Zadie (a cute little mini-labradoodle) kept barking to go outside so I got up to let her out. Getting back into bed in the same manner I had been doing for weeks, I somehow dislocated my hip. The slightest little slip deep inside my hip was comparable to the same pain I felt when I broke my ankle years prior playing soccer. Every time I moved even a quarter inch it was that pulsing, shooting pain through my hip. I found only one position that provided relief, but I got locked into this position sitting in bed with my legs straight out sitting up at a 45-degree angle with my hands behind me for support. I tried to get out of bed, but I was stuck.

    I did not want to freak out my folks since they were at the movie, but after an hour stuck in position, I called my dad and asked them to come home. In the meantime, I called my local orthopedic for advice. He said you may have dislocated it. You need traction or a trip to the ER. Dad called the neighbor, and he came over pronto. He held traction for ten minutes (which is basically putting a little pulling pressure on the leg by grabbing the ankle), but not much relief. My folks came home, and Dad tried again. Minimal relief. We had to call the ambulance. The EMTs

Breaking the Silence

had to come into the bedroom and put the board under me to get me onto the stretcher.

The ER doctor decided the best thing was to try to put it back in the socket. I woke up in the middle of the first attempt of three because they did not give me enough anesthetic. I tried to tell them. People just cannot comprehend my pain tolerance level. I do not blame them, but many times I suffer the consequences while they are on the learning curve.

I had to stay overnight since they could not get the hip back in place. The next morning we spoke with the weekend orthopedic, a graduate of University of Arkansas Medical System like my orthopedic at Mayo Clinic. My Mayo orthopedic decided it was too risky to attempt to put it back in socket with the possibility of damaging tissue or nerves so we elected to wait until the permanent hip surgery, which was late April, about five weeks away. I was not happy with that decision, being stuck with a dislocated hip, but what could I do?

Managing with pain meds and limiting my movement, the pain eased as the days passed. I endured the dislocated hip until surgery. We traveled to Mayo—again that ten-hour drive. We went a few days early for the routine preparation. The plan for phase two was to do two surgeries. Day one would be about twelve hours for the hip implant, and day two about six hours with the rods and screws drilled into the spine to support the implant.

The morning came. I was relaxed having about twenty-five surgical procedures already. We did intake as per normal, and they wheeled me into the operating room. The anesthetist gave me the first pop of fentanyl to help me to start fading out. We were discussing where to put in the epidural in my lower spine, and she was about to do it. Someone over in the corner kind of yelled, asking me when the last time I had blood thinners. I told them last night with all my other medicines and vitamins. I thought that was an odd question since they already checked twice during intake, had a phone interview weeks before, and also had to go through an online questionnaire to confirm all my medications.

After about thirty seconds, the room became very quiet, and it felt like no one was around. I was not sure if I was dreaming since I already had some anesthesia. My head orthopedic surgeon came up to me, grabbed my hand and said, "Trent, we cannot do surgery today because of the blood thinners." About that time, he got a call on his mobile and left the room. He came back and said there was concern there may be a blood clot in my hip. Priority one was to have an ultrasound and verify no blood clot prior to surgery. I asked a few more times for surgery from different angles, but it became apparent that we were not having surgery even if there was verification of no blood clot.

    I could feel about thirty eyeballs staring at me while I lay there half knocked out. The intensity in the room was heavier than a wet fire blanket. I calmly said, "Well, sometimes things happen for a reason, and you do not know why at the time." I could feel the air come back in from everyone holding their breath. There was a massive coordination effort required for all the specialists and nurses needed for my surgery. It takes months to get it booked. I knew the surgery was not going to be rescheduled for a time in the next few days.

    They wheeled me out to a pre-op room and did an ultrasound. Of course, there was no blood clot, so I rested for a bit, put on my clothes, and went back to the hotel. My orthopedic surgeon requested we have an appointment the next afternoon to discuss the future surgery appointment.

    I thought it unnecessary as I had nothing to discuss further, and I was ready to go home, but I obliged. The next day the orthopedic surgeon apologized profusely. Admittedly, it did cross my mind that I was still on blood thinners prior to the surgery. It is pretty common knowledge that you cannot be on them for surgery. I just thought Mayo knew best, so I never asked. I should have just asked the question. The only dumb question is the one you do not ask, right? He told me that it could have been very serious life-threatening situation, and if they could not stop the bleeding I could have died on the table.

    It was good that we had a few minutes to get to know each other and not talk strictly medical stuff. It was a very fruitful conversation. Looking back, I think that could have been partly the

Breaking the Silence

reason the surgery did not go through, and God just had bigger plans and helped me dodge a life-threatening bullet.

We drove home, and a few weeks later the surgery was rescheduled for July. Bit of a bummer for the delay and dislocated hip (who else would have a dislocated hip over four months!), but I was able to get back in the gym to better prepare for surgery. My new mission was to recover faster and better than anyone expected after surgery.

The two months flew by with the start of summer. Concerts, festivals, and fairs were going on. The surgeries were re-booked for the middle of July, which was just perfect as my brother was in the military and coming off assignment. We planned a family vacation to the Smoky Mountains and would road trip straight from Tennessee to Mayo. I knew it was going to be a tough recovery so I wanted to have some fun while I could.

The hip surgery went well on the first day (sixteen hours) and then the spinal surgery (eight hours) was the next day. Little less than twenty-four hours under the knife over two days. They did well managing my pain overall. On the second day, I was on my feet with the physical therapist. The goal was to sit at the end of the bed. It felt great to get up, and I felt ambitious. We did a small walk that turned into sixty yards. The next day I walked a hundred and fifty yards. Five days after surgery I was clocking a mile around the ward. breaking it up into four or five walks per day. Two days in a row I did a mile, and they decided I was good to be discharged. A week after surgery, and I was out of there! (I would say that is Guiness World Record recovery time. I had to give the next person something to shoot for this being the first of its kind hip implant surgery!).

The ten-hour ride home was tough. especially getting in and out of the car. I was mentally prepared from the previous trips. My motto for this recovery was do a bit more than the day before. In a week and a half, I was back in the car driving ... Don't worry, it's okay. The surgery was on my left hip, and my right foot works just fine for driving. I must have my independence!

All was going well, then one night I was out with friends and started feeling terrible. I had to say goodbye early and woke up

Breaking the Silence

the next morning feeling really terrible like I had the worst flu ... bad headache, achy, and totally wiped out. I was running a fever, which I had not done in years. It teetered back and forth for a few weeks between feeling really badly, to kind of okay. Fever over 102, and then chills so bad I had on long johns, a track suit, and two blankets.

    I tried to go out feeling okay and had to come home abruptly many times just after a few hours because I would suddenly start feeling so poorly again. I was so wiped out some days that I was between the bed and sitting chair only. I did not even have the energy to go downstairs or outside to get some fresh air. I was only dealing with the most invasive, most complex, largest hip implant ever done in the world with never-done-before procedures as well.

    I had a virtual appointment check in with the Mayo doctors and x-rays (done locally and sent to Mayo). The implant looked good. The surgeon was very happy. So was I, and we all agreed my flu-like symptoms were probably my body still in recovery from such a massive surgery. This crud just kept hanging on, so I decided to request a local blood test to check my inflammatory markers. The blood test results were sent to Mayo, but the inflammatory marker tests were missed in the data transfer because this test takes longer to process. Mayo did not see any issues with the blood work since they did not get the inflammatory marker tests, so it was business as usual. A perfect storm was brewing.

    We had an in-person appointment scheduled in October. We made the drive, and it really tired me out. I was so fatigued with terrible chills that evening before. I woke up feeling pretty good, and the appointment went well. All were happy, and we were on the way to a successful recovery. As we wrapped up the appointment, they asked me to get a blood test on the way out. I obliged, and we headed home.

    About two hours from Mayo, the phone rang, and it was the nurse practitioner. She asked where we were. I told her two hours away from Mayo on the way home. She told me my inflammatory markers were seventy-five times over normal. "Your hip could be infected, and we would like you to come back to Mayo," she said. I

Breaking the Silence

told her we were going home and would take care of it locally. She again asked. I said, "Really, truly what would you do if you were me?" She said that she would come back, no doubt. It was serious.

I calmly and reluctantly agreed while the voice in my head was screaming, "No, are you serious?! What?!" I was in utter disbelief. My parents, being the rock-solid people that they were, just kept it cool. We turned around at the next exit and headed back. The nurse practitioner called back as we were on our way back to Mayo and said that I had a hip aspiration scheduled the next morning. If it was showing infection, there is a strong possibility that they would have to do surgery.

"This cannot be happening!" I thought. The worst-case scenario of all is that the hip gets infected, and they may have to take out the implant. The hip implant is a one-shot deal with how all the screws and rods were placed. If they must take it out, then I would go back to where I started, with the short leg and four-inch lift shoe where most people try not to look at it, but it always catches their eye. If they knew my story, they would think I was one of the toughest dudes they have ever seen, but more times than not, I catch that moment of sympathy in their eyes. I do not want sympathy. I just want us all to ignore it like it is not there.

But really, is all this pain, recovery, effort, time, persistence going to be for nothing? A waste ... just wasted faith? Am I a pawn in this horrible game. Am I going to be back on crutches for the rest of my life? As these thoughts raced through my head, I felt the heaviness come upon me, a heaviness of despair, doubt, and disbelief mixed with shock. It was a long two hours back to Mayo.

It looks like I am probably going to have to get back in the ring for another round with this hip, but I am so tired. I do not want to do this again. I do not want to fight this again. I know how hard it is to beat a chronic infection with an impaired leg. How much can a person take? I ask you, how much do you think a person can *really* take? I cannot possibly tell you all the details of this train wreck of a journey in a chapter! The remainder of my journey will be published in Volume Three ...

ABOUT THE AUTHOR

    Trent Brock is an international business owner, three-time cancer conqueror, and best-selling author in *Breaking the Silence: Voices of Survivors Vol 1*. If you want to continue the journey with Trent while he defies all odds, you can find him at www.trentbrockcoaching.com. To add to his toolbox of talents, he is now an inspirational speaker, cancer journey coach, and patient advocate ambassador.

CHAPTER 6

THE DARK LIGHT IN ME

Jaclyn Jereczek

I'm hiding in my closet, and I am scared out of my mind. Santa Claus is trying to kill me. I try to hold my breath in hopes he can't hear me. Will he find me this time? Will I live or will I finally die? I can hear him rumbling down the hall, he is getting closer. The fear grows and the panic sets in. I am trying to stay as still as possible, so I don't make a peep. My head starts to wander with thoughts. Why would Santa want to kill me? I love him so much.

I hear footsteps on the other side of the door. I knew he wasn't going to give up until he got me; he never does. The closet door opens, and I cover my head. All I remember being taught was that if I wore a helmet to protect my head while riding a bike, I wouldn't die. I didn't have a helmet, but I did have my hands and I wanted to live.

The door suddenly opens, and I am caught. He pulls me out of the closet with a tight grip and throws me onto the top bunk in rage. I slam against the wall and try to stay as close to the wall as I can in hopes he won't be able to get me. I think to myself, "Is Santa going to reach through the rails and try to pull me off the bed again?" With fear in my eyes, I scream in hopes someone will hear me or he will stop. My brother is sleeping right below me, will he kill him next? I hope he doesn't, I love my brother so much!

Santa Claus got me, and as he pulled me out of the bed ... I woke up. I was terrified out of my mind realizing I was asleep the whole time. Sometimes I wake up frozen, other times I pull the covers over my head not knowing if it was real life or not. Let's be real, we all know that if we pull the covers over our head, the boogie man won't get us. It's the same theory we use turning off the lights and running up the stairs as if Freddy and Jason were trying to catch us. If you try to tell me you have never done this, I'll call bullshit.

Breaking the Silence

Santa Claus coming after me was a reoccurring nightmare I had growing up. Luckily, I had so many nightmares, I taught myself how to lucid dream. Our brains are absolutely incredible! The themes of my reoccurring nightmares were always based around the fear of death. When people tried chasing me through these elaborate places, I taught myself how to hide, survive, and wake up. Eventually, I was able to control my nightmares so well that I changed the outcome. When I got away, I would wake up so proud of myself for getting out of it.

Growing up, I witnessed domestic violence and endured both physical and mental abuse. I was young when my parents divorced. I knew it was for the best, but it changed everything. My mother's bipolar disorder and paranoid schizophrenia added to the chaos. She had a knack for manipulation, causing divisions within our family and turning some members of our community against my siblings and me.

It was always hard to explain life to my friends. They only saw the good side and believed her. Desperate to survive, I gave up trying to convince others of her behavior and focused on finding joy where I could. Let's not forget my poor choices in coping. There were plenty to choose from. High five if you feel me here. I was the queen of toxic positivity. At times as an adult I drank alcohol to numb, and I had no sense of structure or stability. Disassociation became the star of the show. Despite the challenges, I learned to cope through somatic movement, mainly as a skilled dancer in the bathroom, where I could lock a door and let my mind soar.

As I tell my stories you will see how some of my personality came to be. To this day, dark jokes, being labeled "weird," and laughter brought me immense happiness. The sarcasm and fun banter, however, was passed down generationally and I am welcoming you with open arms if you carry these traits. My family even had buttons made saying "Jereczeks ... we aren't so bad." I'd like to think it's better than "the world's best beer." When I got older, I went for runs on some of my angriest days. Sometimes it worked and other days it didn't. Luckily, in more recent coping strategies, I discovered breathwork. Although it

Breaking the Silence

brought out memories to heal, it gave me a healthy outlet to scream, let my anger out, and has even helped my endometrial and overall physical pain in my body.

    Like all families that endure divorce, our life drastically shifted. I ended up living with my dad and brother from middle school on. I was upset. Out of all my siblings why my brother? I didn't even like him. His hockey bag smelled and, to be quite frank, I think he was adopted (just kidding, I love you with all my heart, Bro!). My dad was able to get the courts to agree to let us move to Wisconsin so he could take a better job. In return, he had to drive every other weekend back to Minnesota so we could visit our mother. To this day, I am impressed at the way he handled many situations with us.

    Most would think a lot of my internal damage was done as a young kid. Developmental wise, I am sure this is true. High school and as a young adult, however, held great significance as well. What I will say is, they add to the pile of stories that eventually played a large role in my CPTSD and generalized anxiety diagnosis.

    Over my high school years, I witnessed my mother going on and off her mental illness medication and her medical list continuing to grow. In fact, recent therapy sessions have brought me back to the days when she lived at my grandmother's house. Not knowing what version of her you were going to get, if she was dead or alive in her room on the weekends when she wouldn't come out, all the medications and pills that were on her dresser—sometimes spilled. The paranoia on whether she was successful at killing herself or if she was just making another suicide threat. The smell of marijuana that lingered, which was later documented as an addiction in her paperwork. Wondering if we were going to get kicked out again for disagreeing with her or doing something wrong.

    Luckily, my dad created a safety plan for my brother and I in case we got kicked out. I will save the more extreme stories for another day. Eventually, I turned eighteen and no longer had to visit. With her illness progressing, I chose to take care of myself and to sever my relationship with her a couple years later.

Breaking the Silence

In December 2017 my mother passed away. I hadn't talked to her for years and my conscious was feeling it. When we went to clean out her apartment, I had the weirdest feeling that I should keep her medical records and other paperwork, so I did. I started to question mental illness. I started thinking about the way she struggled, about the times she tried getting help and making healthier choices, and wondering if there was more out there than I was aware of.

A topic I am still looking to learn more about. Not just from a medical point of view, but from those who think outside of the box. From the trauma she caused, it would be easy to assume I hated her. The truth is, I am now on this mission for her. No one woke up and chose to be this way. From stories I heard, she was full of love. So, what and when did things change? Was there something we missed years prior that could have led to all her suffering? My questions in life are endless, as you will begin to learn. Curiosity and love of people lead my life. If you suffer, my heart goes out to you, I believe in you.

About three weeks later, my dad passed away. The deaths were unrelated, but the stress and emotions built up. I joke that my mom took him with because boy, did she not like him. I did though, he was amazing!

For years my body was screaming for me to get therapy. Just like you ignore your parents at times, I chose to ignore my body. I knew I needed to heal on so many different levels, but I didn't realize how impactful it would be for me. Have you ever been through the court systems and multiple group therapists? As a kid, I wasn't a fan of most of the groups or therapy. Trust me when I say, I understand therapy may not be how you start your journey.

Going back to therapy took time but was ultimately the right call for me. I wouldn't have come back to myself without her help, and I wouldn't be as strong going through my medical journey without her. She is the definition of true beauty on the inside and out and I know she was a major gift sent into my life. She deserves to be honored and celebrated. I started analyzing my relationships with everyone in life, eventually ending a few of them. I learned that I wanted to run from some of the healthiest

Breaking the Silence

environments. They were unfamiliar and I couldn't trust them. I was shown tools on how to help my anxiety, CPTSD, panic attacks, and most important, how to come back into my body after trauma—another thing I didn't see the importance of until my health issues a couple years later.

I was meditating one day and was guided into a forest where we were prompted to visualize a door. In my meditation, I wasn't sure what was on the other side but as I opened it, I walked into a room where I noticed my hands covering my head. At that moment, I realized, I had stepped into my childhood nightmare of Santa Claus trying to kill me. This time, I was alone.

I knew in this moment, from having been in therapy, that my body was trying to tell me something and I needed to stay. I relaxed my body so I could experience what was happening. This time I was watching from a different perspective. It's as if this time I was watching over this little girl who feared everything that had happened. My meditation guided us back out the door into the forest, this time asking us to enter in a different way. I panicked. I didn't know what to do. My mind started to overthink again. I couldn't pick a topic. I reminded myself of something I learned in therapy which was learning how to let go.

I surrendered myself to the experience and suddenly I snapped back through that door. This time it was different. I was back in the same place looking over the girl. I reached out my hand and just as I did, she grabbed it and stood up. I gave her a big hug and let her know everything was going to be okay. I had no clue what was happening or why I did that.

In that moment the whole ceiling of the room changed as if it were the northern lights, and suddenly my brother and I were playing with Christmas toys that I loved. The room suddenly morphed into the most positive, relaxing, happy feeling. We were able to enjoy time with one another by simply playing. It was such a beautiful moment to witness. As I laid there with my eyes closed, I recognized how aware and conscious I was of what was going on in real life. I knew enough to stay and at that moment, I realized I had given myself the love I needed as a kid. It felt so good! Tears were running down my cheeks and I came out of that meditation so

Breaking the Silence

confused. I brought my experience into therapy and as I told her the story it clicked. Santa Claus was my mom, and this was a memory of abuse that I had held. The symbolism of it all suddenly made sense. I haven't had a nightmare like that since, and now when I have bad dreams, I'm very conscious and ask myself what has been going on in my life.

Childhood and trauma can echo into adulthood through your body, dreams, relationships, and self. I thought the nightmare was done yet my memory held it until it could heal. It can show up in the fear of speaking up, feeling unworthy and mistrust. Breaking these cycles takes time. Therapy is my lifeline, reshaping my views and body. Its importance, now clear, guides me in my cancer and prevention journey, fostering teamwork with professionals and others.

On November 5, 2020, I was diagnosed with Stage 0 breast cancer and a genetic mutation called lynch syndrome. I was thirty-one. Lynch syndrome means I am high risk for multiple cancers, colon and endometrial being at the top. I don't mean to brag, but I kind of feel like an overachiever at this point. Something my parents would have never described me as. I was the one who had the gift of gab back then and by back then, I mean I still won't shut up when I get excited. I love to jump into other people's worlds to listen, learn, and network. If you are like me and love to connect with one another, let's chat! Luckily, cancer and trauma made me smarter—there's a silver lining to everything. PHEW! This is where my true journey began …

At the same time, I was told as a preventative measure, to have a hysterectomy and to remove my ovaries due to having Lynch syndrome. I signed the paperwork to have everything removed. I didn't want kids, so why not? Something felt off, though. I started to panic, learned from others' experiences, tapped into my body, and eventually only went through with the double mastectomy with reconstruction.

Despite being cancer-free after all of that, I kept exploring new healing methods, driven by curiosity and a desire for alignment with my true self. At this time, I started working for Breast Cancer Hawaii. On top of that, I noticed cancer was

Breaking the Silence

happening more at younger ages. I knew I couldn't keep removing more body parts, so it was time to take a more holistic approach, from diet, to stress reduction, to maintaining well-being and self-awareness. It's about preventive care, nurturing habits that support me and rallying a support network for life's surprises.

I was ready to take life by its … well, you fill in the blank. But what I didn't realize was how much of a journey I was going to embark on after surgery. Rewriting life, struggling to get back on my feet, going back to more appointments, and in November of 2023, precancerous cells were found in my endometrium. Now, some might see this as another setback. That someone can be me sometimes until I realized that was my inner little bitch, and said, "Nope we've got this!" At times, it's gotten dark, but I can't help to remain hopeful, stubborn, and positive. I don't know if this is a blessing or a curse. I have a head that dreams of the "what could be" and a positive mindset.

Let's talk about how trauma can affect teamwork and relationships. One of my unfavorable moments was when someone told me I could die, and it would progress if I didn't take treatment. I was triggered. I had been through cancer before; I already knew this, but my insurance and doctor didn't cover what I wanted. It was at this time I had to ask myself, "How do I take my power back?" I began to question death more and more. I brought the fear into therapy and remembered I had time. I have been doing "brainspotting therapy" for some time and have been loving it. My therapist had me start by finding my typical brain spot on the fear of death. Eventually, as I was trying to sort it out and get to the root of it, I told her I just wanted to hunch over for some reason. She encouraged me to honor my body and follow the feeling. As soon as I hunched over, it clicked.

This was the same position—minus my hands—that my body went into while I was in the closet as a child. I felt abuse in my upper back. Which side depended on the emotions I discussed. My body harbored trauma, and this was the first connection I had physically felt. I realized, had I lashed out on my doctor over a tone that triggered me, words, or anyone trying to use death as a reason for me to choose a treatment I didn't like, I would have

Breaking the Silence

been speaking out of trauma. Unless I had taken it to therapy, I wouldn't have known. There was a brainspotting session where one of my sports bras fit better after. I felt like I lost twenty pounds in my upper torso after it. I'm still blown away. It released something and I can't explain how it felt. From the posture change to the release I had, it became clear that our bodies harbor things.

I unlocked a new level of healing I didn't see coming. I knew I had been living with high stress in my nervous system. I went back into therapy and told her, "It's important to continue this." I know that stress causes inflammation and inflammation can cause disease. If my body kept stress since I was a child, and I was already at high risk, and I knew our environment and lifestyle played a role, then it's no wonder I got a diagnosis.

My body still fluctuates with inflammation. Did you know our bodies show signs in many ways? Our bodies also hold onto trauma, whether its medical or from other situations shaping our experiences in unexpected ways. By tuning into our bodies, we can unlock healing and rewrite our stories.

It's about reframing our experiences, embracing resilience over panic. Studying our body, clean slating what we think we know, and honoring our unique blueprint to healing. Teaching us how to advocate for ourselves. Setting ourselves up with the proper team of professionals, as well as family and friends that fit our own personal needs. Creating our healthy support system and having the confidence in knowing that no matter what is thrown our way, we can thrive. Conquering fears and habits that may have been programmed as a younger child or memories that were so clearly captured within our body. Changing our mindset and our lifestyle to heal our body.

I challenge you to ask, how do I reclaim my power and shift from fear to living fully? How do the foods I eat, the environment around me, my faith or lack thereof play a role? If you are interested in these questions, I invite you to reach out. You have a unique blueprint that only you can uncover. How beautiful is that?! Healing doesn't have to be so cookie cutter. It can be whatever you make it. With the right imagination and crew by your side, anything is possible. You just have to believe and allow yourself forgiveness along the way. Your past experiences shape the beauty of who you are today. There is no shame in it.

I hope you give yourself the gift of "failing" because that means you have tried. That means you are aware. That means you are *strong*! That means you are capable of so many things that will lead you to your community and a more fulfilling life, giving yourself everything you deserve, enjoying life to its capacity. Most important, enjoy it with the people you love and with people who will help you along the way. I'm not going to pretend it isn't hard at times. Trust me, I struggle, but it is always worth it when you get to the other side.

It's about unlocking a newer, resilient you that you never saw coming. Remembering, no matter how dark the moment feels, there is always a light that remains inside. It's about unraveling your subconscious to allow room for your light to shine. Maybe that darkness is your soul asking for you to step into your power and find your new community. Ones who will stand by your side and understand. I am cheering you on, you've got this. Remember, this is just my story, and the beginning of my story at that. Your story is just as YOUnique and can help *many*. Let's collaborate and see what we can do as a team. We rise together and are stronger together. We were never meant to do this alone. With all my love, Jaclyn.

ABOUT THE AUTHOR

Jaclyn Jereczek is your fun-loving mental health and wellness advocate! From navigating childhood trauma to battling breast cancer, being high risk for multiple cancers, and now facing endometrial pre-cancer, she's here to empower others to learn themselves and to keep going on their healing journey

Jaclyn is on a mission to address health challenges, understanding that our bodies are more than just one symptom and one system, she seeks a holistic approach to healing. Jaclyn is passionate about bridging gaps in our systems. She aims to collaborate with professionals, nonprofits, and survivors to foster connections and identify areas for improvement. Through sharing

Breaking the Silence

her story, she sheds light to the impact of childhood trauma stored in her body over the years. Emphasizing the importance of releasing trauma and reconnecting with our bodies to advocate for ourselves, promote healing, and to prevent disease. She understands that everybody is unique. Find your why, find your blueprint, and have some creative fun doing it!

After jumping into the mental health and cancer realm, she realized lifestyle and wellness bridged both worlds. She saw an ad for breathwork in Africa with the gorillas and knew there had to be more fun experiences out there. She plans to speak up, share her journey, and write another book.

She is looking to broaden her experiences, learning more about ancient remedies such as sound healing, herbs, etc., and bring people on the journey as she uncovers alternative ways to heal our bodies. She wants to spread awareness with other survivors through unique and fun healing events. It's time to get goofy! Whether you are into the arts, adventure, or have something a little outlandish in mind, she welcomes it with open arms. Most important is to connect with others along the way. Community and connection are where her heart lies.

Join Jaclyn's community of resilience and empowerment as she spreads knowledge and awareness by supporting those who want to create and bring their knowledge forward. Together, let's bridge gaps in our systems, uplift each other, and thrive! If you're ready to embrace change with a theme song of "You Ain't Seen Nothing Yet," reach out and join the movement! It's time to funkify your healing!

Scan the QR code to book an appointment with Jaclyn.

Instagram: https://www.instagram.com/jaclynjereczek/
Facebook: https://www.facebook.com/jaclyn.jereczek/
Website: Funkifyyourhealing.com

Breaking the Silence

CHAPTER 7

BECOMING THE WOMAN I CAME HERE TO BE

Jennifer Pearce

Those moments that take our breath away, the ones that transform our lives so completely that there is no way back to the way we were before. Those moments that leave no more space in our lives for our former selves. Those moments that find us with no warning. Just a sudden excruciating, and unrelenting jolt. An explosion that causes destruction to all we have known. Those moments. The ones that come without fanfare, or warning heralding their arrival. Coming to transform us, to break us, to wake us, to poke the alive part of us that lives deep inside of our souls. To enlighten us and evolve us into the places meant for the new people we are supposed to become. The moments that break us wide open so that we can become who we came here to be. Those moments that I am speaking of come carrying cruel and excruciating pain, but also magnificent gifts and wisdom. If you are brave enough to withstand the storm, you may just find yourself living a life you only dreamed of on the other side.

If you choose to use those moments as a catalyst, and a catapult, they can propel you forward to meet that person you came here to be. The story I am about to tell you is one such story. It is my story. I am an ordinary woman, ordinary in every way, but I made a conscious decision to fight like hell after carnage and destruction found my life, and imploded it so exquisitely. I decided to fight fiercely for the woman I am today. I felt her early on in this story. I locked eyes with her up ahead and walked my way through the rubble to meet her. To have her become a part of me. Realizing early on that the woman I would be in the future needed a hero. I became my own hero. Here is my story.

My moment of impact came on an ordinary Thursday night after dinner. No fanfare or trumpets heralding its arrival. My life had been so strange that I hardly recognized it anymore. I was living my life in the middle of a pandemic that was raging around the world. Focusing on keeping my family safe, and more importantly my special needs son who had health challenges for whom COVID-19 could potentially have dire consequences. I was worn out and tired, living under the weight of teaching from home during the pandemic, living amid the pandemic, and living in my troubled marriage. It all started to feel like a nightmare.

    I found out two years prior that my ex-husband was having an affair. He had met her at work, and his behavior had changed so drastically that I could not understand anything about him anymore. He was short-tempered and unkind, and I could do nothing right anymore. When I found out that the source of his ill treatment was an affair, I thought I might die. I had never been hit with something so shocking or traumatizing in all my life. I shook until my teeth chattered as the shock and awe set in, bringing with it so much pain and suffering.

    After my discovery of his affair, we decided to fight for our marriage, going to counseling regularly and giving it a go. However, most of the time in that space I spent looking over my shoulder and feeling sad and anxious. What he had done took over my life. I was horrified about what did, and wondered if I was doing the right thing by giving him and our marriage another try.

    None of that mattered to me at the time as much as fighting through all the horror of it to save our family for the sake of my children. Enduring two years of such extreme conditions in the hope that we would find happily ever after. Feeling that if we did, then it would be worth all of the suffering that I endured. So, on this particular Thursday night he had been outside supposedly talking to his therapist, and our slider opened. I was in the living room and could see the slider from where I was sitting. For as long as I live, I will never forget the look on his face. It was a look that told me that everything about my life was about to change. In the most excruciating and profound way.

    After I sent the kids to my bedroom upstairs, knowing what he had to say could not wait, he told me that his affair had never ended, despite what I thought, and that he was leaving me for his girlfriend. The room began to spin again. I began to shake and my teeth began to chatter again! He reached out and I told him, "Don't touch me."

Breaking the Silence

The look of pity on his face made me nauseated and angry. I was absolutely leveled and horrified. Much of that night is a blur, and it was one of the most painful nights of my entire life. Anger found me first. Just intense and wild anger. Wondering how he could do this to me? After all we had been through, and after having me kill myself and destroy my spirit under the weight of the shadow of his affair for two years. Then, to leave me?

I could not wrap my head around it at all. I was unable to tolerate the look on his face. Not heartache like I was feeling, but pity, and it made me sick. We ended up yelling some. I cannot even remember the words, and soon my anger was replaced by flight. My fight-or-flight kicked in, and I needed to leave. I needed to go for a drive and clear my head. I told him to put the kids to bed and I would be back. I got into my car and drove to a place close to our house and just broke. Sobbing from the deepest places inside of me. From my soul. Completely emotionally leveled in every way by it all and feeling desperate and lost. Wondering how I would survive the end of my marriage. A marriage that had spanned nearly fifteen years and a relationship I had in my life for twenty.

What were my kids going to think and feel? That thought continued to shatter me. I made two calls that night—one to a friend and one to our therapist—and sat in my car and poured my heart out to them, and cried, and cried, and cried until stillness found me. Crying so hard and so long that I found my inner calm again. I came home and he came in from talking to his girlfriend. We stood in the kitchen saying our goodbyes and I began to cry again. Just broken sobs moving through my body on repeat. I felt so small and so broken. Like a little mouse. He didn't shed one tear that night. He had steadied himself so completely, separating himself and insulating himself from the pain, so he could walk out the door.

His lack of emotion that night is something I will never forget. Not even willing to grieve our marriage for a moment with me. He was so focused on leaving and living his new life. What he believed would be his best life. And then he was gone. The door closed and my tattered self stood there in the silence. Standing at

Breaking the Silence

the bottom of the stairs, willing myself to make the climb up to my bed, the bed we had shared all of those years. Before I stepped onto that first step I took it all in. I stopped crying. I was still and aware that this moment was a defining one. I was leaving my life to be measured differently, all of the moments before that moment, and all of the ones that would come after, and then my foot found the first step and I began the walk to my room. I laid down on my side, looking over at his side and cried most of that night. Sleep never found me.

The next couple of weeks were a blur. I went back to in-person teaching, a task I wasn't prepared for. That first year after our separation was one horror after another. I was being treated by my ex and his girlfriend in the most horrendous ways, due to the dynamic he had created. He wasn't allowed to speak to me or see our kids very often. I filed for divorce and my life became a blur of rallying myself to endure all the legal ramifications from the end of my marriage. I was also navigating the pandemic and becoming a single mom, fiercely committing to the healing of myself and my children. It was one situation after another that tested my strength and my willingness to endure getting battered in the storm. Amid all the devastation I also began to feel the most amazing light starting to shine through the cracks of my broken heart. Just magnificent light, and I began to follow that light.

Less than a week after he left, I decided to begin writing a blog, sharing my pain in real time. Taking all the ugly feelings and pain that now lived inside me and finding a way to release them. Like a beautiful pressure valve. The inclination to write that blog was the first gift I was given that changed the trajectory of the story. My blog was real and raw. It was wrought with pain, suffering, and truth. I made a commitment to stand in my truth and own my own story. Not wanting to have folks wonder where my husband went. Wanting them to know what happened.

I maintained the high road. In my writing, and in dealing with my ex, despite the way I was getting treated. I chose to focus on the things I could control early on. Realizing that holding onto the things I could not grip was like clutching razor blades, I learned that relief came in letting go. I decided early on that I got to control how I showed up in this story and so did he. However he showed up or didn't was no longer any of my business. I started to focus solely on who I wanted to be in this story and disconnected from him as much as possible. My blog began to touch lives, and I began receiving amazing and powerful messages of support and love for my children and myself on our journey, and it was like a raft amid the storm I had found myself in. I clung to it for dear life.

Around the same time, I began to exercise. My exercise was born in a moment of excruciating pain. A couple of days after he left, he wanted to FaceTime the kids. I was in the other room and heard them talking, and then I heard her voice. The other woman speaking to *my* children. That moment seared through my soul like the night he left, leaving me feeling gutted and in agony. I made a very clear decision that night that a ton of pain was going to find me in this story. A ton, and there was no way around it, but I had a choice how much of it I showed up for.

I took that FaceTime to go downstairs and run on my treadmill. Again, using it as a pressure valve to release all that pain that swirled endlessly inside me. I ran like my life depended on it, because it did. I never listened to FaceTime again. Knowing that I was never going to yank the phone away from my children and harm them any further than they had been and knowing that nothing good was going to come of my listening to it. So I ran and ran and ran some more. Soon I was finding myself getting into shape and marveling at that fact. I was barely sleeping or eating but I was beginning to feel healthier and clearer than I had in the beginning. It was a way to alchemize the need for control in my own life as all the other pieces fell away. At first, I desperately tried to grab the pieces as they sped past me on either side, but I soon realized that it was futile. Focusing on what I could control and letting go of the rest was the only way.

The kids and I began to seek solace in nature. We hiked every chance we got. We found medicinal power among the trees. Breathing in the air and using the magic of nature as a beautiful salve to heal our broken spaces. I tied my shoes and took the kids many days when I didn't want to. The days I wanted to put on music and stare at the wall. Knowing that once we got there it would be worth it, and it was every time. The kids found the same solace I was finding. They were struggling immensely, and it killed me. I would have endured it a hundred times over to avoid their suffering and the witnessing of their suffering.

My daughter was four at the time, and she began sleeping with me after he left. She would ask me every night if I was sure her dad wasn't coming home for months. Each time the pain of answering that question to her little face cut me to the quick. It made me so angry that he caused all this pain and suffering and didn't have to endure the aftermath at all. The kids were confused about not seeing him very often, so they put on happy faces with their dad, saving their pain for their mama. I was more than willing to help hold it with them. The amount of pain that had found the three of us was just enormous. I marveled sometimes at how much pain I was in and I think that if somebody actually knew they would be scared. I did not have the luxury of giving in to it. I knew it was one foot in front of the other, and one day at a time till I found my way through.

Then this beautiful shift began to happen. My sadness began to dissipate. I had such great friends and family supporting me and listening to me every step of the way. The pain was subsiding, and I was beginning to see how much better off I was without him in my life. Realizing how flawed our marriage had truly been and how sick I had become under the weight of him and it.

The freedom that found me in that realization was intoxicating, and I began to believe that I had the power to live any life I wanted. No limits. That notion ignited a passion deep inside of me and a deep realization that this story was going to change my life. My mantra throughout had been, "I can do hard things." I whispered it to myself endlessly, I wrote about it, I believed it, I owned it. Each and every day. I also began to fancy myself a bit of a warrior.

Early on I had read a wonderful book on divorce and the author had a very candid and easy way with words that spoke to me in those early and dark moments. She said, "You have to train like a warrior through divorce and infidelity because it is a

Breaking the Silence

marathon not a sprint." I took that to the bank and did just that. Believing in myself and my warrior spirit on the treadmill and everywhere in my new life. I posted uplifting content to bolster my confidence. I learned all the new "man skills" around my house: mowing, snow blowing, weed whacking, leaf blowing, all of it.

In each new task I learned, a new part of my confidence grew. It grew in the places and things I thought I could not do until I did them. My ex and his girlfriend would mock me some, and take pot shots, and I paid no mind and continued to rise. I found my tribe forming and focused on my inner warrior and drowning out all the noise. I lost some more people close to me because of my committing so fiercely to my journey and showing up as my authentic self, but I didn't let it get me down. It was a small price to pay for living my life awake and alive. I was no longer asleep at the wheel, instead finding myself driving the car, top down, wind in my hair, and tunes cranking with a big grin forming across my face. I began loving everything about my new life, and deeply committed to healing and evolving past all of what had found me.

I knew early on this story would change my life. I just wasn't sure how, not sure of the vehicle to get me there. Until one day I was on Facebook and I saw an ad for life coaching. I clicked it and the woman was talking, and behind her was a sign that said "I can do hard things!" I knew it was my sign. Life coaching was the perfect vehicle to take my story to the places I wanted to be. I teach fourth grade, and coaching is in line very closely with my skill set. A beautiful marriage of things I am already good at. Running along people and watching them win.

I signed up for a life coaching program and I immediately fell in love with it and became a certified life coach. The program was amazing, and I learned so much. A calling was born inside of me: a desire to transform and alchemize my pain for purpose. Feeling a deep passion to help other women on the other side of infidelity and divorce and find a life they are crazy about. Helping their hearts heal and helping them become visible in their own lives. Reclaiming it all and finding love for themselves. This has been the single most incredible gift I found in this story.

Breaking the Silence

I was finally learning to love myself. Taking all that love I was pouring into my ex and now pouring it into me. Showing up for myself every day. Exercising every single day, blogging, and meditating. All of which I continue to do today. I partake in this magical time of the day, in the early morning, and I give to myself deeply before my day even begins. Consistency is where the magic happens. What you focus on grows, plain and simple. I choose to focus on light, on love, on peace, on hope, on faith, and on so much more.

Since I made the decision to be a life coach, I have been a guest on a podcast. I have hosted a weekly women's series to help women find the gifts I have found and support each other in that. I have coached women walking my walk individually and helped them find their own power and voice. I hosted a women's night and a public speaking engagement, sharing my story aloud for all to hear and speaking my truth in my town. I am in the process of writing my own book, diving more deeply into my story, and sharing it in the hopes that it will help others. I participated in an online summit where I shared my story, and I am just getting started! I have a long-term plan to create a lake side retreat center for women and children on the other side of infidelity and divorce. The retreat center will be designed to help them heal at different places of their journey. It will offer fellowship, yoga, meditation, hiking, and workshops to help transform their lives and journeys, as I have.

As a society, we do not do enough or have enough places to hold people in their pain. Helping a mother who is fighting to make it through her own pain and be a mother to her children should exist in our world. Being a mother while I was shattered was one of the hardest things I have ever done. My children strengthened my resolve and my willingness to fight through every day, but it was also very difficult for me to be my best self for them. It took all my effort and resolve to do just that.

My passion lies fully, in transforming the lives of women. In my married life the idea of being "too feminist" was off-putting to me, I am ashamed to say. I was a wife, and a mother, and I reveled in both, and didn't really feel the plight of women … until

Breaking the Silence

I did. It felt uncomfortable to look at my own needs and seek to have them filled. Today I am proud to be a champion of women and their challenges, and I am absolutely honored to have found myself here.

We applaud women in our society if they are depleted, overworked, underappreciated, and running on fumes. Telling women they should love themselves and be confident, but when they do, telling them to calm down. Women can be anything they want to be, anything, while still being amazing daughters, mothers, wives, girlfriends, whatever they wish to be. In fact, dreaming and finding a place in your own life makes you better at all of those things in every way. Trust me. I have lived in both lives, and learning to love myself finally, after nearly fifty years, and learning to give to myself in my day-to-day, treating myself every day like somebody I love, has had a profound impact on my life.

I hope you felt my passion in this story. I am deeply appreciative that you took the time to read it. It is my absolute honor to share my story in the hopes that it will touch somebody else's life and help them realize that they are not alone. You are never alone, I am always cheering for you. ALWAYS!

ABOUT THE AUTHOR

Jennifer Pearce is a mother, teacher, life coach, and writer from Pennsylvania. Her passion lies in having compassion for the human condition, and watching people overcome adversity in their lives, both as a teacher and as a life coach. She loves to see people WIN in their own lives, stepping into their own power, and becoming who they came here to be! She has found a life she is crazy about after her divorce, and she hasn't looked back. Her passion lies in helping other women find light, hope, and inspiration on the other side of infidelity and divorce. That has become her life's mission through her own experiences. She also feels passionate about living each day intentionally, and being open to where her journey takes her, while helping others with their story. Giving her pain a purpose makes her so very humbled and beyond grateful. She is just getting started and cannot wait for what is next, while loving completely the *now*.

She is the owner of Gratitude Journeys Life Coaching. Her site can be found on Facebook. Her blog and business site are www.gratitudejourneys.org and you can reach her there as well. Jennifer would be honored to run alongside you and watch you win, if that is what you wish to do!

CHAPTER 8

THE WEIGHT OF WHISPERS:

A JOURNEY THROUGH CHILDHOOD

Kandiee Campbell

It was 1973, and I was three years old when I learned the weight of words. My name is Kandiee, and I am an only child in a home where silence spoke louder than words. My parents, once bound by love, now drifted apart on a sea of unspoken fears and buried emotions.

In the quiet corners of our home my mother, Patricia, sought solace in whispered confessions. She would beckon me close, her eyes heavy with the burdens she carried, and pour out her heart as though I were her only confidant in the world. However, I was just a child, too young to understand the complexities of adult worries. Yet I listened with great attention, my small heart heavy with the weight of her words. I did not understand that her problems were not mine to solve, nor did I comprehend the toll they took on my tender soul. All I knew was that my mother needed me, and I would do anything to ease her pain, even if it meant sacrificing my own innocence in the process.

As the years passed, the whispers grew louder, echoing through the walls of our home like a haunting melody. I became adept at navigating the minefield of my mother's emotions, tiptoeing around her fragile psyche with the grace of a tightrope walker. However, with each whispered confession, I felt a piece of my childhood slip away, lost in the vast expanse of my mother's worries. I longed to be like other children, carefree and unburdened by the weight of adult concerns. Unfortunately, my reality was far from idyllic, trapped in a cycle of silent suffering that seemed to have no end in sight. And yet, I clung to the hope that someday, somehow, things would get better.

As the years wore on, my optimism began to wane, replaced by a growing sense of resignation. I had become a mini adult in a child's body, forced to shoulder burdens far beyond my

Breaking the Silence

years. Despite the darkness that threatened to engulf me, I refused to let go of the flicker of hope that burned bright within my heart. My heart, tender and fragile, bore the scars of a childhood spent shouldering burdens far too heavy for my young shoulders. As I grew, I struggled with trying to learn how to prioritize my own needs, wants, or desires over those of my mother, whose whispers still echoed in the recesses of my mind.

My father remained aloof from my mother and her concerns, which he played a part in. This became a vicious cycle for me, caught between both of my parents. This resulted in my yearning more and more for love and attention. I became a people pleaser, bending over backward to accommodate others while neglecting the cries of my own soul. I channeled my mother's perfectionism and was learning to become a perfectionist.

I could not control my inside world, but I could control how I presented things to the outside. Setting boundaries was non-existent. It felt like an insurmountable task, a mountain too steep to climb. I longed for the courage to stand up for myself, to reclaim the security and autonomy that had been stripped away from me. However, the patterns of my past kept me captive, their chains tightening with each passing day.

My mother, though remorseful for the pain she had caused, offered no solutions to ease my suffering. Her apologies fell on deaf ears, drowned out by the cacophony of my own inner turmoil. So I buried my emotions deep within, sealing them away behind a façade of forced smiles and laughter. Thankfully, life had a way of forcing me to confront my demons, to stare them down and slowly begin to reclaim my power.

Before I could do that, I experienced the sting of bullying from the girls in my school. They called me names and said mean, sharp, barbs that cut deeper than any physical wound. I learned to retreat into myself, to further build walls so high that even the most determined person could not breach them. And yet, amidst the darkness, there was still a glimmer of light that kept pulling me forward.

My father Norm, an electrical engineer with a penchant for adventure, whisked our family away to distant lands, where he

Breaking the Silence

would fill the air with the scent of possibility. From 1971 to 1983, Iran, Greece, Saudi Arabia—we hopped from contract to contract, our nomadic existence shaping my early childhood in ways I could never have imagined.

Living abroad was a balm for my wounded soul, a respite from the chaos of my inner world. In foreign lands, I discovered new cultures, made friends who spoke languages I could barely understand, and forged connections that transcended borders. In those fleeting moments of connection, I felt heard, understood, seen. But even amidst the beauty of my surroundings, the ghosts of my past still haunted me.

The whispers of my mother lingered in the corners of my mind, a constant reminder of the battles I had yet to face. And yet, as I stood on the threshold of a new adventure, I knew that I was ready to confront whatever challenges lay ahead, to reclaim my voice and rewrite the narrative of my life. As the years passed, the pain within me grew like a silent storm, raging beneath the surface, threatening to consume me whole. From early childhood to the tumultuous years of adolescence, I found myself retreating further into the confines of my own mind, a shell of the vibrant soul I could have been. The weight of my mother's whispers bore down on me.

Every worry she shared with me crushed my spirit with their relentless insistence. I struggled to breathe beneath the suffocating weight of their expectations, their demands, their unspoken desires. With each passing day, I found myself wondering, yearning for a life beyond the confines of my own existence.

I often retreated into the recesses of my imaginations, seeking solace in a world where pain was a distant memory, where the echoes of my mother's whispers were drowned out by the symphony of possibility. I dared to dream of what could have been, of a life untouched by the scars of my past. However, even in the most fervent imaginings, the specter of my own existence loomed large. I could not escape the gnawing sense of guilt that clawed at my conscience, the whispered doubts that plagued my restless mind.

Breaking the Silence

What rights did I have to wish for a life other than the one I had been given? Was it selfish to long for a reality that existed beyond the boundaries of my own suffering? Despite the guilt and the pain, I couldn't help but wonder. What would my life have been like if I had not been born into a world of whispers and shadows? Would I have been free to spread my wings and soar to new heights, unencumbered by the weight of my mother's burdens? Or would I have been condemned to wander the lonely corridors of my own imagination, forever haunted by the ghosts of what could have been?

As the years stretched out before me, a vast expanse of uncertainty and possibility, I knew that the answers to my questions would remain forever out of reach. I resigned myself to the reality of my existence, a prisoner of my own thoughts, forever caught between the echoes of what if, and the harsh realities of what was. As I reflect on my teenage years, I am confronted with the stark reality of the hurt that I had buried deep within myself. It was a hard time, filled with moments of anguish and silent battles that no one else could see.

In 1985, in California, at the tender age of fifteen, amidst the chaos of my family's dynamics, I experienced a turning moment that would shape my journey ahead. My family and I were traveling to a wedding for an aunt, as I sat in the backseat of our car. I felt the weight of unspoken tension hanging thick in the air. My father's impatience and frustration with my mom's struggle to navigate using a map was palpable.

In that moment, I reached a breaking point. The volcano of emotions brewing withing me erupted in a deafening scream, piercing through the silence of the car. "Stop yelling at Mom!" The words reverberated in the confined space, carrying with them the weight of years of suppressed emotions. Anger and rage coursed through my veins, manifesting themselves in throbbing temples and trembling hands. For the next two hours, a heavy silence enveloped us, broken only by the hum of the engine as my father drove on, silently navigating the roads and pulling off the road to navigate the maps as needed.

Breaking the Silence

    The outburst marked the beginning of the need to release all the anger and stuffed emotions that had years of being suppressed. I teetered on the edge of needing to suppress the negative emotions that were desperately needing to come out with the negative emotions I was still feeling. All the hurt and pain that had long been buried within me needed to be confronted. Throughout my young adult life, these unresolved emotions continued to impact me, casting a shadow over my relationships, and filtering the love and worthiness I struggled to see in myself.
    In college, I found myself retreating further into myself, seeking solace in solitude as I grappled with the complexities of my inner turmoil. Unbeknownst to me, I was engaging in a pattern of self-abandonment, shutting myself off from the world and those around me in a misguided way, attempting to protect myself from further pain.
    I really had no clue as to what I was doing to myself, believing I was protecting myself from getting hurt. It was much later in my life that I came to understand the profound impact of that pivotal moment in the back seat of the car. It was a catalyst for self-discovery, prompting me to peel back the layers of my own psyche and confront all the pain that lurked within. Through therapy and learning tools and strategies, I began to unravel the tangled web of emotions that had ensnared me for so long. This continued for many more decades before I finally discovered all I was experiencing was not normal or healthy.
    In 1988 I went to college and continued to see the long-lasting effects of my mom's words. They impacted my relationships as well as how I saw myself as a woman. I was in a cycle of seeking love and acceptance yet pushing it away. I really did not know who Kandiee was or what I wanted. I did know I wanted the pain to go away. I knew desiring love, enabling me to seek men who were broken and push away men who were genuinely kind and nice. I did not see myself as worthy of love nor did I think I deserved it. I attracted men who were like my parents: emotionally detached and broken.
    This belief impacted my marriage and even my motherhood. I knew I wanted something different for my children.

Breaking the Silence

I was determined to do things differently. I must admit, at first the journey was rocky. I still had pain releasing. Slowly but surely, I embarked on a journey of healing, and I learned I was worthy of so much more than I believed I deserved. I began to learn how to embrace and acknowledge the full spectrum of my emotions. It was a process fraught with challenges and setbacks, but with each step forward, I found myself able to reclaim pieces of myself that I thought I had lost.

The emergence of deeply buried emotions marked the onset of a transformative phase in my life, wherein suppressed feelings began to overflow into my daily existence. This pattern persisted well into my adulthood, reaching a crescendo following the birth of my children in 1994 and 1996.

I was in my late twenties with two small kids. We were a young military family with a volatile combination of anger and alcoholism. My then husband and I had many arguments, and because of his drinking and my erupting anger, it was not a healthy environment. A pivotal moment occurred during my early years as a mother when a heated argument with my husband led to an act of aggression, resulting in a gaping hole in a wall of the modest house we were living in. The incident, witnessed by my youngest child, served as a stark wake-up call, as his innocent proclamation reverberated my unchecked emotions. He would go around saying, "My mommy kicked a hole in the wall." This was the wake-up that I needed to try and find something different.

I had to work to set a better example for my kids. The struggles I had were very real. I was still seeking love, but I was also repelling it at the same time. I was seeking love in all the wrong places and with the wrong people. I would go through a divorce and then pick up the pieces and rebuild. I realized that staying in a marriage that was unhealthy was far worse than going through a divorce. I did remarry and my children began to flourish and grow. I began to see my children begin to smile and laugh. This was missing from the early years of their lives. I focused on how I could improve my life and the kids' lives. I threw myself into being the mom I desperately wanted my mom to be to me.

Breaking the Silence

I did make a different choice when it came to my children. I was not a perfect parent, but I made a point to be there for both of my sons until they graduated high school and went to college in 2012 and 2014. I chose to go a different direction, and I am happier for it.

Again, it would be many years before I truly healed and began to understand that the wounded thee-year-old Kandiee needed to be allowed to be a child, and the adult part of us could handle any problems that presented themselves. I still struggled in my marriage, and I wanted something different, but it was many years later before I got the solutions that I needed to learn. I would go on seeking several degrees in psychology with a goal of a final degree of a doctorate in psychology. I was trying to understand all I had gone through and find a solution to let it go.

My mom and I had a fractured relationship until the last few years before she passed away. I began to stand up for myself and not just take all my mom wanted to give to me. Towards the end, she apologized and was truly repentant for what she had done to me. I came to realize my mom had only done what she had been taught. In retrospect, my mom was forced to grow up too young and she did not know any better. When I realized this, I softened my perspective of her.

My parents both were replicating what they had seen shown to them. Thankfully, I had determination to go a different direction. I still made less than ideal choices, but my kids turned into fine young men, and I have apologized for the mistakes I made with them. All I can do is show my family that I am human and take a hundred percent responsibility for my behavior and choices. I am not perfect, and neither were my parents. They did the very best they knew at the time with the circumstances they were given.

Today, as I look back on this period in my life, I do so with a sense of gratitude for the lessons learned and the growth that has ensued. I am no longer defined by the pain of my past, but rather empowered by the resilience that lies within me. Though the journey is far from over, I walk forward with renewed purpose and a newfound sense of self-awareness.

Breaking the Silence

In sharing my story, I hope to inspire others to confront their own inner struggles and embark on their own journey of healing and self-discovery. For it is only by shining a light into the darkest corners of our souls that we can truly find the peace and fulfillment we so desperately seek. Life still happens and I encounter setbacks, but I am stronger for everything that has happened in my life.

As I traversed the road to emotional well-being, serendipitous opportunities began to materialize, ushering in new chapters of growth and fulfillment. A remarkable milestone presented itself when I was graciously offered the opportunity to co-author a book alongside esteemed author Jack Canfield, with the book's debut unfolding amidst the glamour of Hollywood in 2021. It was during this auspicious occasion that fate intervened, introducing me to a venerable MD and co-author, whose wisdom and support proved instrumental.

Following a candid exchange of life stories, he extended a generous invitation for me to share my journey as a guest on his nationally syndicated radio show. I was not in the space to receive the referral in 2021; it would be two years later before I was ready. In 2021, I was still processing the death of my mom and getting hit with a major health diagnosis at the same time.

In January 2023, I received an email from the CEO of Brushwood Media Network. I was invited to have a conversation about becoming a host of a nationally syndicated radio show because the network felt there was need for what I was talking about and the message I had been working to deliver. The radio show has been an amazing opportunity, and I am able to assist people to learn so they can empower individuals to assist them to master their fears, transform loss, and overcome anxiety so they can unlock a life brimming with joy, love, and the freedom they truly deserve.

Little did I realize at the time, this fortuitous encounter marked the inception of my own radio show, signifying the commencement of a transformative journey towards personal empowerment and the realization of my aspirations. There are so many opportunities that I have been afforded to assist people in navigating life's challenges. I have a profound impact upon people using my voice. This can help them emerge as their best selves in the journey of life.

ABOUT THE AUTHOR

Kandiee Campbell is an experienced grief and transformational coach and the host of the *Awaken Hope Radio Show*. She specializes in guiding individuals through the intricate process of healing from loss and trauma.

Armed with a master's degree in counseling and certified as a Happy for No Reason trainer, her professional background is complemented by personal resilience gained through overcoming her own experiences of loss and trauma. Her purpose is to harness this wealth of knowledge to assist clients and radio listeners in finding peace and resolution, empowering them to cultivate lives brimming with happiness and fulfillment.

Her mission is rooted in providing grief and transformational coaching, fostering an environment where individuals can heal from the inside out. She extends her unwavering support to those navigating the challenges of loss or trauma, with a shared objective of helping them unravel profound peace and resolution.

Her goal is to help individuals master their fears, transform loss, and overcome anxiety, so they may unlock a life brimming with joy and love.

CHAPTER 9

IT RUNS IN THE FAMILY

Leah Hallman

When I started writing this chapter, I found myself getting lost in memories. Before I knew it, tears were flowing down my cheeks, and I could feel this intense pressure in my chest. To discuss suicide seems to be taboo. When I mention to friends and acquaintances about my father and how he died by suicide, I get a look from people. It's almost a look of shame and pity. Not from everyone, but some. I have met people that have lost a loved one to suicide, but I find they have a hard time sharing how they died. I get it, there is a stigma to suicide. Almost like it is contagious. It feels that way for me some days because suicide runs in my family. I have lost my father, uncle, and four cousins over the last twenty-plus years.

I was in my mid-twenties when we lost my Uncle Kay to suicide. I couldn't tell you what I was doing that day, but I can say that a piece of my heart broke. What I do remember most is the phone call and hearing my father on the other end of the line sobbing as he tried to get the words out. I knew when he said, "Sweet pea, you need to come home," someone died, but I couldn't imagine who or under what circumstances.

Uncle Kay

Our family lost many generations to death at an early age from auto accidents and other strange accidents, but suicide was a new experience for me. Especially when it was a beloved member of the family, who always seemed to enjoy life, and was full of laughter and love. I was thinking these thoughts as my dad told me how he found my uncle, and how "Kay" took his own life.

I was living in Florida at the time, loving life by the ocean. My favorite part of any day was taking a book or a fishing rod and heading out to listen to the waves crashing, maybe catching a glimpse of a dolphin, or catching a fish. These were things that I couldn't do in Dallas/Ft. Worth daily. After this incident, I had to

Breaking the Silence

leave this beautiful place I loved and go back to Texas to take care of my dad, to be with him in his time of grief.

My memories of my uncle are of a happy, loving man who had a beautiful family whom he loved. Who enjoyed hunting, fishing, and spending time with family. Not of a man who would take his life.

Growing up our family went to Colorado most years during elk season and spent a week or two camping. I loved coming out of the camper and having my grandma waiting with a hot chocolate for me. The snow was thick on the ground, and you knew you were going to make a great snowman that day! The kids played around the campsite while the men and some of the women went out hunting. I remember trick-or-treating at each family's camping area. How fun it was to wear our costumes and have a campfire going and tell ghost stories. These were wonderful times spent with my family, especially my uncle. He always seemed so happy and at peace.

We also spent many years visiting my uncle's lake house in west Texas: boating, fishing, jumping off the dock, and swimming for hours. I can still smell the wonderful food cooking in the background while we sat around in lawn chairs sharing stories. I find myself thinking back on all these moments and my heart aches because he is no longer with us. So many family members are no longer with us.

I am not sure what year he was diagnosed with cancer, but I know from conversations with my dad that it was taking its toll on him. If you know anyone who has suffered from this disease, you know what I am talking about. Cancer breaks down your body and your mind. The treatments are worse than the disease itself, in my opinion. My dad told me that my uncle was not sleeping, his appetite was almost nonexistent, and he had been suffering from depression for a while. I believe all these contributing factors were what led a loving, gentle, happy man to take his life. My father told me many times that he believed the sleep deprivation that my uncle was dealing with daily was most likely what led him to do it.

Breaking the Silence

Cousin Jack

It was years later when my cousin Jack took his life. It would again break the hearts of our family. Inevitably the questions started. "Did he leave a note?" "Do you know what was going on in his life?" "Has he been suffering from depression or using drugs?" Throughout the years, these same questions surfaced after each tragic passing.

We were not close as I grew older. I left west Texas in my late teens and rarely traveled back, if I could help it, but I always loved and enjoyed his company when I was a kid and teenager. Cousin Jack was funny, enjoyed great music, and loved cruising around in his Camaro. My grandma Pearl adored him, and I adored her, so I adored Jack as well.

Some things I remember about him most are silly things: his crooked smile, boisterous laugh, long hair and beard, even as a young man. He looked like a hippie rocker, and he loved music. I can still picture him driving up to Granny and Gramps place in his Camaro, windows open, music blaring, and a big smile on his face. After all these years, I still cannot remember a time he was not smiling.

I remember one summer we spent the weekend at my Uncle Kay's lake house. We were sitting around in lawn chairs after a day on the water and suddenly you heard loud rock and roll music and the sound of a car's engine coming around the corner. Driving up with a huge smile on his face was Jack jamming to J. Geils song "Centerfold." I must have been around nine at the time, but I came running to his car with a smile. I loved that song too! I crawled in the passenger seat, and we drove around the lake until the song was over.

I remember the phone call from my brother Mike relaying Jack's passing. How he had done it and where. I won't go into the details. I don't like to think about that. Those are not the memories I hang onto.

My Father

Labor Day weekend has always held a special place in my heart. Well, ever since my son was born on Labor Day, anyway. I

Breaking the Silence

got to choose the date I went into labor due to health issues I was experiencing during my pregnancy, so when the doctor gave me a few different days to choose from, I thought it was perfect to go into labor on that day. Many years later I came to dread the holiday. I got sad, depressed, but more importantly angry on the days leading up to it. Some years it would overshadow my son's birthday.

One Labor Day weekend my boyfriend Howie and I spent hanging out with friends and neighbors at his place. We were smoking briskets and ribs to share with our friends. It was a good weekend, for the most part. We ate great food and hung out in the pool. Unfortunately, Labor Day itself was a disaster. We had a car wreck late that afternoon when Howie lost control of his Corvette and hit one of those large square neighborhood mailboxes, the kind that holds around twenty of your neighbors' mail. Anyway, you can imagine what hitting that mailbox with a Corvette did to the Corvette. I suffered whiplash and had a headache, so instead of seeing my dad that evening I spoke to him on the phone several times and let him know that I would see him the next day and bring him leftovers.

He seemed to be in good spirits. He told me that he was in pain and had run out of his pain medicine. He suffered from rheumatoid arthritis as well as spinal stenosis. He was scheduled to have surgery for the latter in a few weeks. I knew he was struggling with what was going to happen after the surgery. He was going to be staying at an assisted living facility for a few months after the surgery for recovery and physical therapy. I could not take care of him like he needed. He was a large man, and I didn't have the strength to move him, and help him with necessary day-to-day living while he recovered.

I knew that he didn't want to go to an assisted living facility. I think he felt that if he went, he would not come out and live on his own again. Losing your independence can be very difficult for people to handle and my dad was no different. I think he was upset that I couldn't take care of him, but I was raising a teenager, working full-time as manager of a plant nursery, and going to school full-time at night.

Breaking the Silence

The morning of September 4, Howie drove me to my house on his way to work. We were still upset with each other over an argument we had over the weekend, and I was still feeling very sore from the accident. When I arrived at my house that morning, I phoned my dad to let him know I was coming over around lunch time to bring him leftover barbecue and go by his bank and deposit money for his medications. While we were talking, he said he was eating Malt-O-Meal and watching the news. We spoke about the argument my boyfriend Howie and I were having, and he told me I should not let the disagreement cause us to end things. My family knew Howie and his family for years and my dad cared for him and knew he was a good man to have in my life.

My son and I were living at my mom and stepdad's house during this time. They were wonderfully supportive of my desire to return to school and helped me out, so my son had someone home with him at night and on the weekends as I worked a full-time job and attended classes four nights a week.

The morning after Labor Day changed my life. After my conversation with my dad, I then went to lay down. I believe the time was 8:30 a.m. I felt pain in my neck, head, and heart and thought crawling into my bed and wrapping myself in the covers would do me wonders. I needed to rest and clear my head before running to the bank and seeing my dad for lunch.

Around 11:30 a.m., my stepdad knocked on my bedroom door and told me someone was at the house needing to speak to me. He had a strange look on his face and asked if I was in trouble. I didn't understand why until I walked out the front door to see an officer standing there. I was as confused as him. Then I thought about the fact that we hit a mailbox the day before. Howie and I spoke to the police after the accident but maybe they had additional questions.

I invited the officers in and asked them if they needed more information regarding the incident and they looked confused. Then they mentioned my dad's name and asked me if I knew him. I was a little taken aback. "Why would the police ask me about him? Was he in trouble? Had he had an accident while I slept?" I had all these thoughts running through my head like a hamster on a wheel.

Breaking the Silence

I remember my mom walking into the living room at the same time the officers suggested I take a seat. The look on her face told me she knew what they were about to tell me. How did she know when I couldn't possibly imagine it?

I was still in my sleeping shorts and top, hair a mess from just waking from the nap. I wanted to go take a shower, get myself clean and presentable and go see my dad. I did not want to sit here and listen to what this officer was going to say to me. I knew it was bad and I didn't want to hear it. I wanted to see my dad! I didn't want to have a seat and listen to this man, but I sat. I listened. I listened as he began to tell me they received a phone call from my dad a couple hours earlier and he told the dispatcher he was going to take his life. He was going to use a gun and they were going to find him in the bathroom.

He told them he had locked the apartment door deadbolt and the privacy lock, the lock that has no key on the outside of the door, so anyone unlocking the deadbolt could still not gain access. I had a key to the deadbolt. He didn't want me to show up for lunch early and find him myself. He explained to the dispatcher he would leave the sliding glass door open so they could gain entry there. He told them I was coming, and he wanted them to get to him first, notify me of what he had done before I found him.

One of the things I think about from that day was that I did not cry. I sat there listening to the policeman narrate the 911 call, telling me my dad was dead, that he took his own life, and how he had prepared it in a way so I would not find him first. I had no tears, just a blinding anger he had done the one thing he promised me twelve years earlier he would never do to me and my son. The tears would come soon, but right then it was just anger! Red hot anger because he left us in this manner. Left us on purpose!

My mom had left the room at some point and went to her bedroom. When she came back out it was to tell me she had phoned Howie and he was on his way. The policeman told me my dad had left a letter for me and after they processed the scene and concluded their investigation, they would send it to me along with his effects.

Breaking the Silence

Then he was gone. Just like that. He walked into our home, changed my life forever, and walked out the door. Strange that I as watched him leave, I was thinking these thoughts of how a person can come into your home, give you devastating news that would change your life forever and just walk out the door like it was just another chat. I believed at the time he should have stayed. To see the fallout of what his words had done to me. Irrational, I know, but if you are going to shatter someone's world, you should stick around to see the fallout.

I called my best friend Deena and told her what happened. She was able to take a bad situation and bring sunshine to it. I remember going to my room to change clothes. I could not wear the same clothes that I was wearing when the policeman changed my life. I needed to be clean and fresh. I went into my bedroom and sat on the bed smoking cigarette after cigarette until Howie came. I didn't realize I had started crying until he was holding me and brushing away the tears.

Later that afternoon I was allowed to enter my dad's apartment. Thanks to my boyfriend and stepfather, they made it presentable for me. I needed to be there, amongst his clothes, furniture, bed, etc. I could feel him there amongst his things.

In the aftermath of his death, my life changed. I became depressed and spent time hiding under the covers. I ended up leaving my management job a few months after my dad's passing. I had a hard time getting out of bed. Eventually, I pulled myself together, started working full-time again and went back to school. The anger stayed. I had grief, good memories, and some understanding after I read his suicide note, but the anger stayed.

When my Uncle Kay took his life, my father promised me he would never do that to me. He would never take his life and leave me devastated like we were after my uncle's passing. He knew firsthand the pain and suffering that those left behind would feel, and he said he would not want to cause me or others that kind of grief. The anger, I think, has stayed with me all these years because of the promise he broke. I have moved on, have wonderful memories of our time together, and I'm grateful for that time, but still somedays the anger resurfaces.

Breaking the Silence

Cousin Jay

As I mentioned earlier, my family has suffered many tragic losses. Good people die far too young. When we first received the call that Jay had passed away there were several conflicting stories as to what happened. Some said he died of a drug overdose, some said suicide. I couldn't picture my cousin Jay taking his own life. Not the Jay I just began to know in the last few years. The Jay I knew loved life, made beautiful woodwork, and was trying to get his business together. I didn't know Jay very well. He was my cousin, and we may have met when I was a kid, but I didn't really *meet* him until I was in my late thirties.

Cousin Jay was my paternal uncle's son. He was raised by his mom, and it wouldn't be until we got older that I would see him at his dad's house for family barbecues and really got to know him. I know it brought great joy to my uncle to have Jay around, especially after Uncle John lost his youngest son Danny in a traffic accident.

John and Danny had a strong bond. The love they had for each other was evident from the first day Danny was born, and John held him. I could write a whole chapter in another book about those two, but what is relevant to this story is after Danny's death, uncle John wasn't the same. A few years after Danny's death, uncle John would pass away from health complications. I think he just wanted to be with his son again.

So, Jay lost his half-brother and his father in a few short years. He was "heartbroken"; those are the words he spoke to me. He told me after his father's passing that life was getting hard again and he missed them terribly.

Maybe this contributed to his actions on that fateful day when he took his life. Maybe it was a combination of that and other problems I was not privy to. What I do know is that a sweet young man with an infectious personality chose to leave this world by his own hand.

Cousin Gray

It was hard to write this last story. My young cousin Gray was the same age as my son when he left this world. He truly had a

Breaking the Silence

kind soul. He was the type of person that embraced everyone and helped any friend or stranger in need. He was full of kindness and love.

His talent on the guitar and his love of music is what I remember most. He was in graduate school when he chose to move on from this earth. He was a classically trained guitarist and musician, and when you heard him play, he would leave you awestruck. I watched him get lost in a song and sometimes it seemed like the music was flowing out of his very being.

The last time I saw him was the weekend we buried our grandmother. I remember him getting up and speaking at her service, and I could feel his anguish over losing her. It was very hard to watch. I do have a great photo from that weekend of him, in my grandmother's living room, wearing a pair of her clip-on earrings. I took the photo because he brought laughter to us during a very difficult time. He also brought out his guitar and played for us while we were eating. It was beautiful music that was meant to bring joy to us all.

I drove him and his mom back from the funeral to my home a few hours away. I will never forget that night driving. We were all singing at the top of our lungs to all the great classic rock songs our family has always loved. We sang till our throats were horse. It was a lot of laughter with great music that was much needed after the burial.

We stayed up late talking about different topics, but one thing I remember vividly was him saying that his heart was broken. I wasn't sure if it was from a girl or from the fact that we just buried our grandmother, and he didn't elaborate. I wish now I knew the answer to that question, because just a few weeks later he took his life.

The morning I found out he was gone, his mom had phoned me and said he was missing. He attended school out of state so it was not like you could just go down the road and check on him. I was in the process of loading up the animals and getting on the road for our move to Florida. When she phoned me back an hour later, it was to say that he had been found.

Breaking the Silence

I still think about that two-day drive, the tears I shed alone in my truck with just the kitty to keep me company, and the fact that I couldn't go be with his mom right then. That was one of my many regrets.

Over the Years

I don't like regrets. I had so many over the years. Wishing I had said this or did that. Did I miss something about my dad? Could I have saved him? Did each of those family members we lost exhibit signs of what was to come? What demons were they dealing with? Could we have helped?

To this day, I still don't know. What I do know is I loved them and all I loved about them. I help friends and family when they need it and let them know I am available to talk or help anytime.

I don't shy away from speaking about suicides and my experiences and feelings. I am very open to questions about how I have coped with the losses, and if I feel I could have done more. I want others to know that they are not alone.

I encourage others to get help for a friend or family member if they are suffering from depression or suicidal thoughts. If you even think they are contemplating suicide reach out and encourage that person to speak to someone about their feelings. There are so many great resources out there for families and friends to access for those they love.

ABOUT THE AUTHOR

Leah is a mother, wife, and a survivor. She is finding her voice to speak about the tragic deaths of her family members and is working with others who have faced similar tragedies. This was the first time she has written about her experiences, but after the writing of this chapter she plans on writing and speaking to others in hopes of saving a family from having to experience the pain she has suffered. She has been invited to speak about her experiences on podcasts and looks forward to this new chapter in her life. She also supports her cousin Gray's foundation, www.Graesynfoundation.org, which helps kids away from home in college get mental health services, housing assistance scholarships, financial assistance, and more.

Resources:
https://988lifeline.org/
www.nimh.nih.gov
National Suicide Prevention lifeline-1-800-273-TALK (8255)

CHAPTER 10

ONE IN SIX

Andrew Cook

Before you read this story, I have a few requests. These requests seem straightforward now, but they might become challenging as you read on. They help me stay grounded and maintain perspective when I retell my story, and I hope they provide the same effect to you.

First, remember that everything is okay in the end. The story is still evolving, but the outcomes are worth the journey's suffering.

Second, this story isn't about good or bad people but about sick and healthy people. There may appear to be villains, but everyone deserves compassion. Bishop Desmond Tutu, in *The Book of Forgiving*, provides excellent wisdom saying, "What about evil, you may ask? Aren't some people just evil, just monsters, and aren't such people just unforgivable? I do believe there are monstrous and evil acts, but I do not believe those who commit such acts are monsters or evil. To relegate someone to the level of monster is to deny that person's ability to change and to take away that person's accountability for his or her actions and behavior."

We must remember that we are dealing with people. People who can change, if they choose to do so, and people who are accountable for their actions if we choose to be brave and tell our story.

Finally, remember that much of this story is a historical event. Many things today can remind me of that time, but there is no immediate danger. You may also feel that pieces of my story remind you of an unsafe time in your past. Be brave and remember that today, we can do for ourselves what others did not do for us in the past.

Before

I don't remember much about the period before my trauma. My parents were married and had their expected share of ups and

Breaking the Silence

downs. I grew up in the "latchkey kid era," where I was alone for long stretches of time, even at an early age. My father worked a regular nine-to-five job, except I remember him being gone before I woke up around 7 a.m. and didn't return until close to 7 p.m. He almost always came home in an exhausted and irritable state. I was used to hearing, "Don't disturb your father; he has had a hard day."

My mother worked odd hours at a church, including several evenings and weekends. She would sometimes take me with her, but nobody kept an eye on me. The lack of supervision led to many incidents, one when I leaned back a little too far and ended up falling into the toilet, getting stuck with my knees and armpits up, as if I were in an inner tube floating down a river. I stayed there for some indeterminable amount of time until a stranger happened upon me and rescued me. I was scared, embarrassed, and covered in toilet water. Another incident was when I located scissors at my mother's work desk and gave myself a rather unflattering haircut. There were many other moments, but these were two that my parents found endearing and brought up often. Rather than viewing them as indicators that I could not care for myself at the ripe old age of four, they treated me as an odd little adult who made poor decisions.

My parents scolded me for being too loud, messy, and a constant inconvenience. I understood my father to be angry and that I was responsible for his frustrating life. These interactions started a pattern of beliefs that told me I was in control of how my parents felt, and that it was imperative to avoid making them angry, upset, disappointed, or sad.

While other kids attended afterschool programs or spent time with friends, I returned home to an empty house due to strict rules prohibiting socializing on school days. Alone, I ate whatever I could find and watched TV for hours, becoming so familiar with *Star Trek* that I could identify episodes immediately. Content with the only situation I knew, I couldn't understand or manage my loneliness.

My parents demanded that I be self-sufficient, responsible for waking myself up, feeding myself, bathing, and keeping the house tidy from a young age. These rules taught me to figure things out independently, avoid bothering my parents, and strive for perfection to prevent disappointment. This drive for perfectionism didn't push me to achieve; instead, it kept me fearful of failure, avoiding new challenges and staying unnoticed. Consequently, I grew uncomfortable asking for help, creating a significant barrier to communication and connection.

Sometime before I turned eight, my parents started attending parties with church friends. Occasionally, these parties involved other couples bringing their kids, but I mostly remember the early gatherings being adults only. My parents would task me with cleaning the bathrooms and other duties to prepare for guests and then ask me to stay in my room and out of the way. These parties had interesting themes and games, and my parents put a lot of effort into cooking food for their guests. For a child, listening to everyone having fun and knowing there was food I wasn't allowed to eat while sitting alone in my room was torture. I ached for someone to see me and include me. The adults-only party rule changed once my parent's friends, Bev and Bob, decided they would adopt children.

Bev, a librarian, and Bob, a schoolteacher, had wanted kids for years. I remember Bev as a stern woman, every bit the stereotype of a librarian who would shush you if you talked. Bob was a big teddy bear of a man. He was an ever-smiling school teacher. The kind of teacher that students visited into adulthood and reminisced about fondly. When they announced that they would start fostering children, their community of friends, my parents included, were thrilled. I don't remember much about the conversation details, but I can still remember seeing my mother happy in a way that wasn't normal. Her normally calm and subdued demeanor was lively, excited, and almost manic. It was as if she found out she was the one getting a new child.

Once their first two foster children, Mark and Sam, were situated, my mother made it her mission to install me as their new best friend. Sam was about my age. He had thick Coke-bottle glasses, had a nervous habit of flicking his chin with his thumb, was obsessed with getting rich, and had a lot of difficulty making eye contact. Mark was three to four years older but only a grade or two above me in school. He was blond, athletic, and mischievous with impeccable manners. In many ways, these two boys were opposites—Sam being the object of much worry about "fitting in" and Mark being the model child. I remember being reluctant to fill the friend role, but my mother insisted and reminded me that it was my duty as a good kid and church member to welcome these new boys into our world. My mother manipulated me by describing how Mark and Sam came from a bad home and that this new life with Bev and Bob was an excellent opportunity to experience something better: loving parents and friends, stability, and a supportive community. Even as a young kid, I appreciated how those things sounded important, and I had no real power to say no. I wanted to please my parents to avoid conflict, so I reluctantly followed this plan.

While Sam never changed, it wasn't long before I saw the dark side of Mark. Over the years, I watched him set fires, torture and kill family pets, lie to others about things I had said and done to create drama, and gaslight adults about the source of chaos that followed him around. Mark had a way of knowing what you cared about and ruining it. When Sam was allowed to own gerbils, Mark would pull off their tails in front of Sam and then threaten to kill the animals if Sam squealed to Bev and Bob. When Mark was later allowed to have pet rats as a reward for his responsible behavior, I watched him set them free in his room and then kill them with a blow gun he made from a section of pipe and some thin nails wrapped in tape, laughing and yelling "Got him! Oh man, did you see that?!" I didn't understand all of what Mark could do, I just knew it wasn't safe to be around him.

Around the time that I became aware of Mark's more disturbing character traits, I began to protest any efforts to visit Bev and Bob's house. My mother became irritable, expressing her disappointment for having raised an ungrateful and unkind child who wouldn't try to befriend children whom she felt were deserving of a better life. I didn't have the words to explain what I had seen and experienced. I didn't know how to tell my mom that it was scary to watch Mark torture pets or how humiliating it was for Mark to easily persuade others about cruel things I did not say.

Breaking the Silence

I had lost friends and felt ashamed that others believed me to be so unkind. I didn't want to be around Mark, and said, "I don't want to go." This was the strongest argument I knew how to muster.

Many months after my parents introduced me to Mark and Sam, their church group started to have parties where everyone brought their kids along. Suddenly, there were many kids at these parties. The part of me that was lonely and scared relished the idea of more kids to play with, and I remember thinking that maybe this was a way to get away from Mark. It didn't slow Mark's devious behaviors, despite more people being around. He was a great manipulator and worked hard to draw a line between those he had some power over and those he did not.

So, while there were many kids at some of these parties, Mark decided that only the "cool kids" would hang out in Bob and Bev's bedroom while the others would stay in the basement and watch a movie. The bedroom had a waterbed, and Mark made it a game to jump around on the bed while Sam and I were bounced about by the waves. It was at one of these parties that Mark first molested me in front of Sam. I recognize now that Sam wasn't shocked and made no effort to tell anyone what he had seen. Whatever threats came with the gerbils were nothing compared to the threats that accompanied this sexual abuse. Not long after, it was another party where he first raped me. Soon after that, he forced Sam and me to abuse each other. This pattern continued for roughly three years. I was sure that my parents learning about my participation in this sinful activity would land me in a kind of trouble I couldn't even imagine. I could see no path out of this existence, so I didn't resist.

Eventually, the church group stopped having parties. I assume this was the result of Mark attempting to abuse one of the other kids and the group fracturing over rumors and resentment. I wasn't part of this conversation, but something changed the dynamics suddenly. My parents stayed friends with Bev and Bob, and at some point, my mother started talking to me about how Mark was creating problems in the home. His violence and abuse were too much for Bev and Bob to manage, and while I was still around Mark at times, I was no longer left alone with him. I believe my mom thought Mark and I had a special friendship and that allowing our friendship would somehow be his salvation from the bad things he was doing. I don't have any other explanation for why she knew Mark was dangerous and still brought me around. She didn't know the extent of the harm he had caused, and I had no way to tell her. Bev and Bob took a great deal of interest in me for years and years to come. I thought they were just nice people at the time, but I suspect they knew the danger and chaos they brought into my life and didn't know how to say sorry. They believed they made amends by taking an interest in my life, but it wasn't enough.

    About the time my abuse stopped, my parents had my brother. Without knowing what happened to me, my parents saw my erratic behavior and believed they had done something wrong with me. Because they saw me as a failed experiment, they tried to raise my little brother very differently. As if I was a lasagna that accidentally got burnt because someone forgot to set the timer; my parents felt that nothing they did would save me. They started over and paid more attention to my brother.

    I don't remember what my brain was like before those years. I am keenly aware of how my brain changed due to those events. I became angry and anxious, and I was in the early stages of an addiction to drugs that I used to numb my pain for decades. These changes in my personality happened to line up with puberty, and so my parents saw me as a hormonal and ill-behaved creature to largely be avoided.

    I hurt myself by cutting. I snuck drinks of hard alcohol and prescription cough syrup, and eventually used drugs regularly. I experimented with methods to numb my anxiety and pain. I didn't know how to identify it or locate it, and any activity or substance that produced general numbness or unignorable momentary pain was a welcome escape when I could find it.

    I struggled to maintain friendships because I didn't trust others and developed hypervigilance that kept my head on a perpetual swivel. I was sad and withdrawn from my family. I screamed at my mother and threatened her with a knife when she tried to make me go to church. I didn't want to hurt her, but it was the only way I could set a boundary to protect myself. My grades were terrible, and I got angry when teachers brought this to my attention. Socially, I pushed my support network away, and I was struggling.

My parents gave up. I mean, they really gave up. They stopped trying to enforce consequences for my actions and rarely engaged me in any conversation about my behavior. The tables had turned as they wanted to avoid me as I had once attempted to avoid them as a child, believing that by ignoring the worst of my behavior, they could avoid feeling discomfort.

Throughout my early adult life, I continually sought help from mental health providers. I knew something was wrong but didn't have the words to explain it, nor did I trust any counselors enough to tell them this story. I would seek help, and then at some point in my treatment, I'd decide that we weren't making progress, thank them for their time, and quit. They couldn't adequately help what they didn't understand, and I swore I would never share the piece of me causing such misery.

In my sophomore year of high school, I started dating a young woman who later became my wife. After six rocky years of on-and-off dating, it looked like I had my act together, and we married one year after I joined the military. If not for my wife's desire for our marriage to work, my self-destructive behaviors would have never come to light. When we tried counseling to address the chaos I was causing in our marriage, enough of my story came out for a counselor to take effective action. Once revealed, the counselor referred me to a twelve--step program and a new counselor who worked with people with my history. He was the first person I ever told my whole story to. It was amazing how giving a provider all the pieces enabled them to help me effectively.

Even with the problem identified, I struggled for almost a decade, making small bits of progress and then relapsing or falling into old, unhealthy thought patterns that kept me stuck in a rut of my own making. One of the best things I did was entrust my wife with my story. When I created problems, she understood the source of my pain and self-loathing. She didn't let me off the hook because of it, but it helped her see me as a human struggling against something monumental. As Bishop Tutu alluded to, she gave me accountability with grace and endured the worst of who I was for the promise of who I could become.

Now

    As an adult, I can see how this perfect storm had to exist for my abuse to occur. I needed to be isolated and lonely, to have parents who were absent and didn't listen, to be at an age where hormones and sexuality were new and challenging to interpret, and to live at a time when "stranger danger" was a more significant concern than who was in the next room.

    The statistics tell us that one in six men have been sexually abused or assaulted, with the majority of occurrences happening before the age of eighteen. Five independent studies between 1990 and 2005 confirmed and reaffirmed this statistic. Even so, these statistics are probably very conservative. Males are far less likely to disclose than females, and only 16 percent of men experiencing sexual abuse so severe that it was caught and documented by social services consider themselves abuse victims.

    Men with this history of abuse are at greater risk for mental health disorders like PTSD and depression, alcoholism and drug abuse, suicidal thoughts and attempts, problems in intimate relationships, and underachievement at school and work. You can look back through my story and see how my journey involved most of these things. While underachievement might have been something I experienced in limited quantities—like flunking my high school algebra class—I also had periods where I overcompensated for my internal sense of worthlessness by overachieving.

    The warning signs of sexual abuse may not be immediate and obvious. Common indicators can vary wildly. There isn't a right or wrong way to be a victim, process your experience, or cry for help. I tried hard to be normal. I often didn't want to be seen. I could hold myself together for a while and then be out of control with no obvious link to those years of abuse.

    Mister Rogers has a beautiful quote: "Anything that's human is mentionable, and anything that's mentionable can be more manageable. When we can talk about our feelings, they become less overwhelming, less upsetting, and less scary. The people we trust with that important talk can help us know that we are not alone." I can appreciate this wisdom as an adult, but it was not my childhood experience. I did not feel I had people I could trust with that important talk when I was a kid. Talking about these experiences, even today, can feel dangerous.

Part of the complexity of this story is that my abuser was a male. He was not homosexual, nor have I ever questioned whether I was heterosexual. In a society that was, and continues to be, fixated on sexual orientation, this part of the story can feel like diffusing a bomb. How do I even explain an experience that was both scary and had all the positive physical sensations we expect from sexual activity? I've been thinking about that point and have no clever analogy or way to make someone understand that experience. It is important to acknowledge that my abuse is not about sexual orientation. The story wouldn't have changed had I been homosexual or if my abuser had been. The sexual nature of my abuse is distracting, but we must focus on the abuse itself: that cruel treatment of another person involving physical force for a bad purpose.

At eight years old, I had certainly not been given any sex talk by my parents. They eventually got around to it almost a decade too late. I didn't have words to describe what was inflicted upon me. The abuse happened in a way that might have made me appear willing. I didn't fight. I was too scared to resist once in that vulnerable position.

Threats of pain can be used to control, but my abuser never threatened me, nor did he coax me. He acted as if it were a foregone conclusion that things were happening as they should. As a child, I accepted the situation I was in. As I looked at it, there was "proof" that this was supposed to happen. The abuse occurred when many adults were nearby, and my parents insisted that this relationship was good for my abuser. Consequently, I watched this abuse happen to others who also did not report it. It would have been more unusual if I had raised a red flag.

Breaking the Silence

Consider the following as a comparison:
- My parents bring me to play basketball,
- Sometimes I get hurt,
- Sometimes I feel good,
- I assume my mom knows about the game because she brings me to practice and tells me how friendly my teammates are.

It doesn't seem reasonable to report under those conditions, does it? My young and immature mind registered the situation like basketball practice.

Part of my healing journey has involved being the adult in my life that I needed as a kid. I give myself permission for this to be painful. I forgive myself for not being strong enough to stop the abuse and being too scared to mention this tragic human experience for decades. I was a kid, despite what my parents believed, and I didn't have the resilience to handle those events at the time.

As an adult today, I have invested heavily in my healing and recovery. I've sat through hundreds of hours of counseling and thousands of hours of twelve-step meetings, and I've had thousands of hours of unpacking this story with my wife of twenty-five years. My adult self is taking this journey seriously and stepping in to protect myself and others, which I could not all those years ago.

My parents continue to be friends with Bev and Bob, despite knowing the abuse I suffered while in their care. I maintain a conflicted and distant relationship with my parents and ask that they not speak to me about their time with Bev and Bob. They are my family, but they have never regained my trust, and I remain guarded around them. Though we live minutes apart, I see them only a handful of times per year to maintain boundaries that protect my psychological safety.

The Future

My wife regularly works with sexual abuse victims, both adults, and children. Though I don't hear the specifics, I see her and her coworkers become the trusted individuals Mister Rogers spoke about, trained to address the unspeakable and advocate for justice. I'm grateful these victims have someone who hears and believes them, a resource I lacked growing up. While this support is crucial, I know the victims will still face a lifetime of confronting their trauma.

Starting the conversation is the first step toward healing. I want other victims of sexual abuse to know they don't have to remain stuck in a place of discomfort. We can replace unhealthy coping mechanisms with genuine resources, find and trust supportive people, and confront our abuse without fear or judgment. The journey is challenging, and support is essential. We may relapse into old habits, but that doesn't make us weak. The path to healing is unique for everyone, and we must embrace patience and acceptance for our journeys. If you are a survivor in need of support, or know someone who is, I recommend reaching out to malesurvivor.org or accessing resources on rainn.org.

ABOUT THE AUTHOR

Andrew's journey from confusion and silence to understanding and advocacy is a testament to the resilience of the human spirit. As a male victim of sexual abuse, Andrew represents a story seldom told in the open. In a society where such experiences are often shrouded in silence, the prevalence of this trauma among men remains largely unrecognized. Statistics reveal a startling truth: one in six men has experienced sexual abuse. Yet, this reality's unique challenges and consequences are frequently misunderstood, dismissed, or outright denied. A lack of understanding and acknowledgment leads to insufficient care and unresolved trauma, affecting millions of lives. His narrative is a powerful reminder of many men's unseen struggles and the urgent need for a compassionate, informed response to their experiences. By speaking out, Andrew aims to bridge the gap between silent suffering and the path to healing. He believes his voice can inspire other men to break their own silences, seek the support they deserve, and embark on their journeys toward recovery.

CHAPTER 11

THE SNIPERS WE COULDN'T SEE
Karen Comba

The final patient of the day was being dismissed from our dental practice when the phone rang. "Are you alone?" asked the voice. I barely recognized that it belonged to my dad.

"No," I replied.

His voice shook, but it got louder and firmer as he asked the question again. "Are you alone?"

My heart was in my throat. "No, what is it?"

His voice changed to a scream, like none I had ever heard. "Your mom did it."

I knew right in that moment what he meant. Mom had taken her own life. She'd carried out her threat. "She's still warm. Help me ... who ... what ... do I need to do?"

I couldn't help him. I couldn't do anything. I felt life drain out of me as I hurled the phone against the wall, hearing the ding as it broke into pieces. An agonized, primal outcry of pain and protest let loose. I was losing time, losing my mind, losing my strength. I pictured myself in my dad's arms saying, "Why didn't I stay?" The guilt of leaving my mother shrouded me in cold darkness. I had spent the morning with her and planned on coming back that night. I was twenty-nine years old, a motherless child, lost in the repercussions of mental illness.

My mind started to drift back in time like a movie of our lives, this time in color. I saw myself looking at my mother feeling excited, "Can I hold the baby or maybe touch the baby?" As I looked into my mother's eyes, I couldn't understand the cold, dark grey color as she just stood there holding my new baby brother, glaring at me. No words were spoken, not even a gesture from her body to mine as she turned and walked away. This memory was the first unwanted feeling I experienced with my mother. I had no way of knowing what was happening and how confusing and scared I would become. I recall the chill that ran through my body, I was just four years old.

Breaking the Silence

Standing as if I were frozen, I looked down and saw my little dog. Coco just looked at me and I saw how her eyes were warm as she looked at me with pure love. I was so confused about what I did wrong. Why did Mom look at me that way? I had no clue what life's path had chosen for me. I picked up my little Coco and went outside and sat on the step. I felt my eyes fill up with tears. This was the beginning of the end for my mother and my relationship, I just didn't know it.

One afternoon when we were little, all of us kids were playing in the yard when suddenly, Mom came screaming out the front door as loud as I had ever heard her! "I told you to take your sister and brother on the west side, you damn dumbbell! You goddamn dumbbell, you play on the west side of the house! Can't you see the bullet holes on the house?! They are shooting at us!"

As Mom went inside, I snuck up to the east side of our house and I looked at the little chips of paint that had fallen off; I couldn't see any holes in the siding. I wondered who was shooting at us and when they did it?

I started to try to hide from my mother. I always thought that playing in my room was my safe place. One day I heard my mom coming up the narrow squeaky stairs, so I hurried and slid under my bed. I could hear her shoes walking across the wooden floor and then the covers went up and I could see my mother's eyes glaring at me. Then she started poking me with the green broom handle hard into my side. The pain was almost so shocking I didn't know where to go and I screamed and started to cry. "Get out of there, you dumb ass! I am going to beat you! I know you are going to make friends with those people outside!"

I couldn't think. "Who was outside?" I thought. "I don't know who you're talking about," I said.

She replied, "You get a different shirt on, you know not to wear yellow!"

I kept trying to move away from the stabbing of the broom in my side and my legs. I finally slid out and tried to run past Mom. I felt the blow to my head as I made it to the stairs and slid down the narrow steps as fast as I could go to get ahead of her and get outside. I ran so fast and made it to the barn and went into the hayloft and hid. I don't know how long I was there. I just stayed till I heard my father's pickup in the farmyard coming. I started for the house and Dad said, "What are you doing, did you have a good day?" I loved him so much. I wanted to tell him, but Mom was standing in the doorway with that glare, and I knew I better not say a word.

This was my life till kindergarten started in the fall and then school became my salvation ... at least till 4 p.m. when the school bus dropped me off. I was the target of my mother's illness. The strangest thing was no one talked about it. No one said anything. Sometimes my uncle or grandma came over and talked to Dad in the kitchen. "What are we going to do with her?" It was like they would whisper, and I just wished someone would talk with me, tell me.

I never knew what would set my mother off and make her my "scary mom." I found myself hiding in the attic a lot and climbing outside my bedroom window and sitting on the roof. I could hear her yelling, "Where are you, you damn dumbbell?! You're so dumb, wait till I find you!" I would be so quiet so I wouldn't be found. There were times I lost the battle and Mom would find me and the beating began. It was like she was trying to beat a demon out of me that only she could see.

I wanted to feel happy like all the kids I saw in school. I lied one time, and told the bus driver I was supposed to get off the bus with my girlfriend at her house. I told my friend that my mom said it was okay. I wanted to see how their house was. I went inside and it looked like a normal home. I asked my friend, "Where do you hide when your mother hits you?" I will never forget her look.

"My mom doesn't hit me," she said. I just looked at her and at the age of eight, I couldn't understand. Suddenly, I saw my mother driving into their yard. I was so frightened. My friend said, "You better go now." As I met my mother at the front door, I could see the glare and darkness in Mom's eyes, "Get in the car, you damn dumbbell."

As we got out on the gravel road, the car stopped, and my hair was being pulled so hard pain shot down my body. Mom pulled me out of the car and then I saw what looked like a tree branch. Before I knew it, I felt it hit me on my back and I fell to the ground.

I could hear some of the vulgar words ... "You are dumber than a barn door. I don't know where you came from, but it wasn't from my side, you dirty little bitch of a liar. I will make sure you think twice, dumbbell, before you run away again! You goddamn shitass." Then my brain did a funny thing; I couldn't feel anymore, and I couldn't hear the words. I just started running for home. I could hear the car as it came up behind me, but only when I heard the door slam that's when my world went silent.

As I grew into my teenage years, issues with my mother's daily episodes were still prevalent, just different. My mother kept telling me, "Don't bring home a papoose or I will beat the hell out of you, and I won't raise it." I started to date a neighbor boy. He had no clue about my mom, and I never shared my secret. One day Mom had a strange look on her face, somewhat mean. "Get in the car!" As we drove into town she pulled up in front of the medical clinic. "Let's go!"

I followed Mom into the clinic, and we sat down. It was a small town, so the lady knew who we were. The door opened and the nurse came out and called my name. "Karen, come on back." I looked at Mom and I wanted to scream, "Why are you making me go back there? I don't feel sick!" The glare in her eyes meant I had to go or face the music. I went into the room and the nurse handed me an open-front robe and told me to take my clothes off from the waist down. She said the doctor would be in soon. My eyes filled with tears, and I asked, "How come?"

"You're getting a Pap smear so you can we can put you on birth control pills as your mother has instructed."

I stared to shake inside. "Why are you doing this? I am only thirteen, I don't understand." I did what she said but I was wanting to scream to someone to help me. I didn't know why my mother was doing this. My God, I was so terrified.

Suddenly, the room went blurry, and the doctor came in. I don't remember how but I could hear the nurse saying, "Here is the instrument." Again, I felt cold air on my skin and then pain inside

Breaking the Silence

my body and burning. Then, just like when mom would hit me, I learned to not feel it. I took myself there—the grass was so tall, and the beautiful smell of wildflowers filled my head. I kept taking deep breaths to smell every flower and I heard the wind blowing through the grass. It was magical.

I remember looking at the ceiling and asking God in my head, "Why?" I was in a cloud of thought when I heard my name in a louder tone, "Karen, you can get dressed." I leaped off the table and put my clothes on so fast. I went to the waiting room and looked at my mother with her cold glare and I wanted to scream at her, but the words were locked inside. Did my mother want me to have sex?

It became a Catch-22. I wanted to feel needed, and I wanted a hug so bad, and I needed to feel that someone wanted me. I used the pill to try and give me what I wanted. The sad thing was, I would have sex and I would still feel so empty and dirty.

I found myself staring in the mirror sometimes and not seeing myself. I continued to try and fit in. You know teenagers: drinking, smoking, whatever everyone was doing, I did it too. None of my girlfriends even knew my life at home. In school I never heard what the teacher was saying. I would just watch the clock, and when the bell rang, it was time for me to go home. I never knew which version of my mother I would get. I always was ready for the "dumbbell" or the harsh words. "You can't belong to me because you're so stupid." Or a hard hit to the head. Or just the glare with no words spoken. I kept my secret and manipulated my friends so I could be with them as much as I could. I didn't want to go home.

Graduation came and everyone was going to college except for me. I heard my mother yelling in the kitchen, "I am not spending any money on a child that is that stupid, what a waste!" I wanted to go to college so bad. I wanted to go with my friends. I was so hurt and felt so dumb and isolated and lost. I had no idea who I was supposed to be. So, my life was planned by my dad wanted to get me out of there. I ended up being shipped off to Professional Dog Grooming College clear across the U.S. I was scared to death. At the young age of seventeen, I was on my way to

Breaking the Silence

Oregon. Instead of just giving up, I was determined to be the best at dog grooming.

I ended up graduating at the top of the class and received a beautiful award. I was so proud and thought maybe my mom would see I wasn't dumb. When I got home, I had a vision that Mom would hug me and tell me how much she missed me ... even though I had been gone over three months and had not received one phone call from her. I opened the door to the car and Mom looked at me; my heart went right into fear mode—the glare was still there.

"What the hell have you done with your hair!?" I ran to find my dad. He hugged me so hard and said he missed me. It seemed to help with the pain I was feeling. After returning home from dog grooming school, it became clear when I walked in the house I was no longer welcomed back. My mother had gotten rid of all my things from high school and put a few things in boxes in the closet. The bedroom was my sister's now, and it was at that moment that I felt my heart breaking. I wanted to cry but the tears would not come. The next thing I knew, Dad was helping me find a job in the paper, a job a hundred miles away. I could tell Dad loved me, but he had to find me a place to go. It was best I leave.

I found it to be so lonely, more so than I had ever felt. I didn't have a home to go to and now I was living on my own. It was good that I grew up fast. I was like an old soul.

As life would have it, I met a young man at work, and we began to date. I didn't realize how lost I was. I was subconsciously wanting attention, someone to care about me. The signs were there but I chose not to see them. Once he hit me on my head, I instantly went back to the feelings of when Mom hit me. The strange thing is, I took it and stayed. I married him even though there were no feelings of love for him at all. I needed to feel wanted and I wanted to have a baby. I never told anyone, but I felt if I had a child it would belong to me, and I would always have someone that loved and needed me.

There was abuse in our house. I kept looking past it. I had two children, and I started to see this human for what he was. We had moved and were farming with my father when I witnessed his

Breaking the Silence

verbal abuse to my father. That, I found out, was the thing no one was allowed to do. It crossed my line. I immediately divorced him. I wasn't sad. I had my kids and that was all I needed. I took classes and became a nurse's aid, and all was well.

As life proceeded, I met a new man and we started to date. My father was joyful. He seemed like a great guy. We married and then he adopted my children. It seemed to me like this was a perfect fit. My children were so happy. I still lived by my folks so I would take my mother to her monthly psychiatrist appointments. Mom was on multiple drug medications for her schizophrenia. The drugs seemed to make her look like she was in a daze and very sleepy all the time. I guess they felt this was the only way to get her through; just drug her up.

I never said anything to anyone, but occasionally I saw Mom look at me with that spooky dark glaze and I could see her wanting to say or do something to me.

I never shared with anyone that my husband was turning me into a Barbie doll. To the extent of telling me how much I could eat and what I could eat. This was a new kind of abuse. Total mental game. I couldn't believe how bad I was feeling about myself. He had me doubting my decisions and my feelings to the point I was making myself sick. Something was starting to happen to me.

I was getting angry!

I had been abused physically and mentally my whole life; I was starting to rebel. I started hanging out with girlfriends and going to the kids' events at school. I was not going with this man to his rodeos to watch him perform anymore. I was no longer interested in his hobby. I was learning and making myself learn the books to the business so I could possibly go out on my own. I stayed till the children were almost adults and then I knew I had to leave. I thought I had my shit together. I had no idea that I was unravelling and self-destructing quickly. I could tell something was wrong, but I couldn't stop it.

I did the unthinkable. I left my son who was going to be a senior, my daughter a freshman in college, and I ran away. I knew

Breaking the Silence

I was breaking down in my mind and I didn't want them to watch. I wasn't sure I would ever be okay.

I couldn't believe I allowed another man to walk into my life with controlling and mental abuse. Something inside kept saying you must fight back and make a good life. I hurried and entered real estate school and studied my butt off. I let the abuse keep going just so I would have a roof over my head. Some part of my mind was working hard to achieve my goal, but there was a part of myself that was gone. I couldn't feel anything, it was like I was empty inside. I couldn't handle it. I was feeling so confused, and I knew I was messed up to some degree.

I somehow passed my real estate exam. I started to find my way. I escaped the freak and found a place to live. I felt peace in my apartment with no one there, just quiet. I started searching for myself. I would see my children as often as I could. They did not realize they were saving my life. I was hanging on by a thread just for them.

I was resilient and saved money to afford my apartment. I would eat at the real estate office because there was always food. I learned to pretend so Mom wouldn't hit me. I now pretended in front of all the other agents that I was somebody and passed off the successful image. I made friends with another realtor named Larry, and we became close first as friends, and then we knew something was special. He went back and met my children, and they all got along great. I was still not sharing the dysfunction inside my head with anyone.

We were planning our wedding. Out of the blue, Larry had a massive heart attack in my arms and passed away. My mind exploded with grief. I felt alone and lost and drained of all the strength I had. I almost gave up. Friends kept pushing me to keep selling real estate, keep fighting for my family. I kept up the front and was financially making it and sending money to the kids for college. But inside at night, I would die. I would drink to fall asleep and get up and do it all over again the next day. Finally, Larry's folks convinced me I needed to move near my friends. I felt like I had a new beginning even though it made us all sad I had to leave.

Breaking the Silence

I landed a great job. No one knew my past and how mixed up I still was. I would work and go home and mentally die again. I found myself asking, "How can I keep going?" I had a fire inside of me that said, "You will show your mother you're not dumb!" I was determined to prove to the world I wasn't stupid. I kept up the front and all seemed good.

One day I was introduced to a gentleman everyone said was a great guy. I was drawn to him. We married and then, out of nowhere, this spooky personality came out. He stood outside and stared at our apartment. He would stare at me and not say a word. I realized I was with someone that was more than crazy; he was dangerous. I ran in the dark one night, scared to death of him, and ran into my neighbor. I told her what I was witnessing, and she helped me get connected to people to get an annulment and change the locks. I felt he was going to do something to me even after that. I found him stalking me and called the police. Somehow, thank God, it ended.

No one at work knew. I had to keep my job and I was getting promoted. At night I thought to myself, "Was I still living in fear and doubting myself because of how I was raised?" I started slowly thinking I couldn't love anyone but my kids. I needed to start finding out who I was. Could it be I needed to start loving myself?

I started my long journey to find myself. I made close girlfriends that were divorced like me. We started walking at night, five to seven miles. I started eating healthy, but to be honest, I still had to drink myself to numb the pain inside. It was my quite little secret. In the world's eyes I was doing well. I thought I had made my life successful. My children were battling their lives and finding their way as young adults. I thought maybe this was it. I was okay if this was just the way it ends.

You know how the world goes, God closes doors, and He opens others. Well, He was about to open my door wide open! My old friends said, "You are going to Denver, and we are attending 'Coloradoans for Nebraska' for the football game at the Fox and Hound." GO BIG RED! Since we were from Nebraska and die-hard football fans, I said, "Why not?"

Breaking the Silence

I was feeling so good with myself. I had learned to love myself. Then this man walked into the room. I had never in my life, with all the men I had met, ever felt lightning hit my heart instantly. I couldn't move and I asked my friend, "Who in the holy Jesus is that?" My angels had come and said, "It's your turn to feel love so deep in your soul you will understand how your dad stayed with your mom even through her sickness."

Friends of my mother tell me how incredible, fun, and giving she was to anyone in need. She loved her family and fell head over heels in love with my father. I still find myself sad that mental illness robbed my siblings and me of the joy of having our mom well. Mom, I will not let your life go down in vain. In your honor, I promise to fight for families like ours.

ABOUT THE AUTHOR

Karen Comba has dedicated her life to mental health advocacy for children. She, alongside a team of incredible people, are putting together program solutions for children. Karen is wanting children living in a home with mental illness to become a high priority. To get the word out faster there is work being done to bring her story to the big screen.

Karen is on a nonprofit board that will bring awareness and recognition to people doing amazing work behind the scenes. She feels that she was chosen to do this work. Karen is a wife, mother, grandmother, and to many, a friend. Karen will continue her work until God tells her she's done.

Website: www.karencomba.com
Instagram: karencombawrites
LinkedIn: karencomba
Facebook Group: Karen Comba Mental Health Advocate for Children

CHAPTER 12

LOST AND FOUND:

THE AFTER-EFFECTS OF TRAUMA

Annmarie Entner

    This chapter may be a little bit different from the ones you have already read. During the process of writing, I came to realize I did not have anger in me to facilitate the ability to put pen to paper. That was how I always pictured me writing my story. Anger and disappointment in me with others as my driving force for wanting to write my story. So let me start by saying I come from a place of peace and forgiveness for myself and the players who were part of my trauma. Not only did I realize there were many parts to get me here for peace of mind and appreciating all I have, but I also managed my trauma with grace and compassion for myself to not give up on living.

    Finding love for myself along this journey was one of pain … until it wasn't. The beginning of my healing began with the understanding of where my parents came from and how their trauma affected me. It was not like they set out to hurt me emotionally and mentally, it was just how it was. The bane of my existence for decades was to blame them and their mistakes for all I had endured as a young woman and adult. I am now a mother and grandmother. Looking through different lenses I can see how I continued the generational trauma. Unwilling to see my part, it took a string of many traumas and healing to forgive them. They did the best they could with the tools they had.

    Growing up during the late seventies and eighties was complicated for me at best. My house was full of alcohol issues and not one person was willing to address it on any level. I remember feeling alone in a house full of people who were afraid of their own demons. My parents' marriage was anything but peaceful. My dad worked a million hours, it seemed, and my mother was surviving at best. How does someone thrive in a house filled with chaos, resentment, and fear? I was the youngest and I

Breaking the Silence

was the stereotypical clown. Boy, did I live up to it. Like I said, I am the youngest. My sister, the eldest, was perfect in my parents' eyes growing up. She followed all the rules, was a good student, went to church, and didn't push any of the limits. My brother was the athlete, for whom the sun rose and set. How do you get seen in an environment like this? I did by being the entertainer and getting as much negative attention as possible.

In 1983, life seemed to take a turn and looked like I was going to be a rising star in my parents' life. My brother left for the Army and my sister got married. It was my time to shine with my parents. I was a teenager, making friends, involved in school as a cheerleader in the fall and softball in the spring.

Life changed really quick. My mother had one of her worst drunken episodes and I paid the ultimate price for it. The day started with me being in the St. Patrick's Day Parade, marching with my cheerleading team. I was fifteen and feeling amazing. I met my parents at the Knights of Columbus Hall and my mom was out of control fighting with my dad. The string of events was horrific with lasting emotional scars.

One that I struggle with was my sibling abandoning me and saying, "It's your turn now." It was a hard lesson at fifteen, knowing that I had no one to rely on for help. My mom had one more episode that I managed much differently when my own string of events took off on a life of its own.

That same year, in May, my junior high school was held hostage, ending with the gunman killing himself. Feeling completely lost and abandoned, I told my mom I was ready to move. As if I had any control over that.

They decided to move to change their circumstances and environment. That December we moved to upstate New York, which was in the country, and I wasn't greeted warmly by the locals. I was referred to as the city girl. I was like, "Um, no, I am definitely not that!" I am not a fan of NYC; my dad had many words to describe the city that were very unfavorable.

I graduated high school and knew college was not for me. I was lost and had no direction. My parents were hard on me, and I

Breaking the Silence

believe that was because after my mom's last episode, I became more vocal and shared how I felt about them.

Once again, my life was about to take a huge detour. My parents packed my bags and sent me to live with my sister. This time the abandonment was cutting to the core. I knew that I was viewed as the troubled one. Everyone was pointing their fingers at me, and no one was looking at themselves. Of course, living with my sister was not easy for her and she sent me back to my parents' home. I was in complete overload of how I was going to live my life because no one wanted me. I knew at this point I needed to find a way out. I got a job at a retail store and reconnected with a girl I went to school with. We became great friends, and I could see that maybe I was on a path to success. However, that path was quickly halted.

I was violated in my twenties. Three boys I was friends with came into the room I was sleeping in. They pushed open the door and started to pull my pants down while I kicked and fought to keep my pants on. I blacked out and my friend came in and pulled them off me. I showered and sat on the couch till morning. I got dressed and went to work. My friend and I never spoke of it again and I never thanked her for helping me.

A few months later, I met my daughter's father, and I believed he was my way to get away from my parents. I can say looking back, he was the first person I gave my heart to, and for all the wrong reasons. I had this fairy tale idea that everything was going to change. Once again, I was shown that life was cruel. My parents abandoned me again because I chose to live with him. It was the first time I made a conscious decision to live my life on my terms. We welcomed our daughter eighteen months after moving in together.

Three months after that, I had emergency surgery to remove my gallbladder. My parents were now back in my life because they were excited to be grandparents for the second time. They were there when I had complications and was in the ICU. They were great, and it was then that I softened and thought we all were going to have a great relationship. Shortly after, I began having difficulties in my relationship with my daughter's father, and we had many heated fights. Our last one ended with him hitting me and I left, never looking back. Not knowing where I got the courage to leave him but knowing that home was easier than finding my way alone at that time.

Feeling broken, scared and alone, I existed for the next few years in a state of confusion. I was not able to get out of my own way emotionally or mentally. I joined a support group on the suggestion of my sister. It was really a way to get out of the house, as I was kept on a short rope and controlled by family members. I was trying to raise my daughter and nothing I did was correct, or so I was told by the one who had no children and threatened on a continuous basis to report me for child abuse, wanting to take me to court for custody. Constantly living in fear, I obliged to all their requests.

I met my future husband during all of this, and it took us thirteen years to make a commitment and get married. Really how can you have a successful relationship when you are not even having one with yourself? Hindsight is 20/20, right? After I married the man of my dreams and had everything I wanted in life—house, husband, daughter—I believed this would make me happy.

I now see life through a different lens. I had it all despite all the trauma I experienced. I still felt broken, scared, and alone, plus a complete mess emotionally and mentally.

My daughter was the one who "saved me." She was able to see that I was on a path of destruction. She needed to get out or be kept a hostage like I was at her age. Generational trauma is so real and I was continuing it by not really addressing what was the root cause of mine.

My daughter took me to court and became emancipated so she could get away from me. This is what I tried to do with my mother, but my daughter accomplished it. We both were mandated to see a therapist, and this is when I chose to look really hard at all the trauma that had happened to me.

Truth be told, at forty years old I was ready to end it all. I had a plan on how that was going to look like, and it was going to be quick. At least that was how I visualized it in my head. My husband was traveling a lot, so I had lots and lots of time to think about it. Not only was I thinking this, I was seeing a psychotherapist in which I never shared my thoughts of ending it all. Why would I share? She would have to put me on a psychiatric hold? So, I embraced the pain laying on a couch three days a week, crying and crying and reliving my past. Looking at it was very difficult. I had no coping skills nor was I able to live without them in my life. I had been to therapy for many years, and finally after twenty years, I spoke about being violated.

Dr. Bell and I started from the beginning, and I let it all out. Why not? I had a plan. I told her everything from having a shitty childhood to admitting myself into a mental institution, not once but twice, and of course being violated. I wrote letters to everyone in my family about how I felt. "You all abandoned me and left me to fend for myself with such anger and disdain for all of you." She read them back to me and those letters sounded like a teenager screaming for help, wanting someone to love her. Who would have thought writing letters to those that had hurt me would help? Well, it did!

She had me write to my daughter and all I could write was, "I am sorry." Sorry for not being the mother she deserved, the mother I wanted to be, and sorry I drove her away. I knew my part and I knew she wanted no part of me, and I had to let her go. It was the hardest thing I had to do, and it still is to this day. After years of therapy, three days a week, and not ending it all, I wanted to live.

I asked if I could start going one or two days a week. Her response to me was, "No." That's not how therapy worked. I went a few more times and stopped going all together. I had enough tools that I developed over the years. My main one was journaling. I could write for hours when I needed to get myself out of a funk, and that worked for years … until it didn't.

I had one more breakdown in 2016, and what was different that time was that I asked for help. All the therapy I had done had a lasting effect.

This time it was different. I was on a journey to move forward and put my past in the past, knowing it is a part of me but not who I am today. I decided to go all in with a psychiatrist, a man (Dr. Morrow) who believed in not just giving me medication but talk therapy too. I met with him for three years. He would give me homework and I would do what he asked. One of the assignments was to read the book, *The Four Agreements*, and I still go back to it to this day. I will pick up this book and read it. and each time I read something new and incorporate it into my life.

    My biggest lesson and question I asked him was, do I have a story to tell and if so, I would like to pursue it by becoming a life coach and giving back. He was my second biggest supporter at that time and said I was capable of anything. Right after I asked him that, he asked me why I was still seeing him. I told him, "Because you told me to be here." He responded that working with me was a pleasure and it was time for me move on with the tools I had developed in my sessions. I stared at him in shock. After all the years I went to therapy, he released me and said to live the life I wanted.

    I left not knowing what that was until a few months later. I heard a woman on her podcast say I can change my life by changing my thoughts and can create the results I wanted for myself. It blew my mind. This podcast had me hooked from just that one statement and off I went to create. Unfortunately, I still had no idea of how to do that, so I joined her women's weight loss group and followed everything she said. More shocking, I had no idea what story I was telling. I spent the next year totally engrossed in her group and making positive changes.

    I had a belief system that I was not allowed to enjoy life because of all the trauma I had endured. I wanted to be loved and liked by everyone and I put everyone but myself first. I wanted my daughter back in my life and had no idea how to change the outcome of the past. While working on all of that, I realized the only coping skill I had was journaling. I was keeping all those beliefs alive and well, repeating what I believed to be true. when in fact my traumas were circumstances that happened to me. My thoughts around my traumas and the false narrative I had on repeat were paralyzing.

Breaking the Silence

This was when I got my first life coach and boy, did it change everything. She questioned my thoughts and asked if what I believed was a fact or a story that I was telling myself. I was telling myself a story 95 percent of the time. In learning this information, I decided to get certified as a life coach and be the "Why Coach," because I struggled with why I could not find my why.

I was asked to come take care of my dad, as my mom made the decision to put him on hospice so he could pass comfortably. I had to put my certification on hold as he needed me and I was unable to figure out how to balance care for him, my mom, and myself. However, the gift I received was so much greater at the time and I had no clue …

COVID-19 was in full swing, and life was on hold for everyone except the dying and their caretakers. The little bit of knowledge I gained from my few months of getting certified became my foundation of distinguishing facts and stories. This was when my parents and I started to move past the past and into the present. My mother put complete faith in me to care for my dad till the end. We spent many nights talking together. There was so much peace between us, and he gave me and himself forgiveness. My dad's words, "You are a good girl, you are kind, and you are strong," will forever be a grounding moment for me. In fact, I write it in my journal as I start each entry.

This opportunity was given to me to show how I am all those descriptions. I watched my sister unravel in her emotions when losing my dad, my daughter showed up as a granddaughter, and my mom as the vulnerable wife. These were roles I had never seen before, and I was the strong one. I remember having a last moment, knowing my dad needed to hear. "I got Mom, go peacefully knowing she is in my care."

Struggling with our new relationship, my mom and I faced the challenge of me becoming her caretaker. I was aware that her health could deteriorate rapidly, considering how little she had taken care of her COPD during the years looking after my dad. I then had a front row seat watching all her fears surface while we healed our relationship.

Breaking the Silence

My mom died three years later, and I was at ease knowing she and I were in a good place ... until I found out about the will.

My dad told me I was strong. My mother wasn't when it came to facing what finalities needed to be taken care of. She said horrible things about me in the will and it showed just how weak my sister was, because she hid behind my daughter to hide it from me. True narcissism at its best.

At that moment I knew the growth I had accomplished in my life. I allowed myself to be angry and feel I never wanted anything to do with that kind of person in my life again. When faced with being emotionally, mentally, and physically abused, I let it slide for all those years.

I learned how to have grace and compassion for myself in a new way. I did not do it alone; I had the help of another coach who had me look at what my saboteurs were and how at one time they were my survival skills. When I dug deep, I saw that I was no different to myself than anyone else

I knew I was abusing myself as well. I broke down each component: the pleaser, stickler, controller, and hypervigilant were the highest on my score. Being a pleaser was my greatest survival skill growing up. It allowed me to be the joker and put everyone first. The stickler helped me be a perfectionist because if I could not do it their way, I was told to not do it at all. The controller and hypervigilant were best friends because in trying to control all my surroundings, I became hypervigilant to keep safe. All of them backfired as soon as I tried to live on my own, and forty-plus years I do not understand how they played a part in my life.

They worked for a while then became my life's saboteur. I learned that with every life experience I had, there was a gift in all of it. Especially when I got diagnosed with rheumatoid arthritis. I showed myself how to live, live in the moment, and not question it. I had lived through a ton of pain and with my arthritis. I experienced physical, emotional, and mental pain at any given moment. I have the power to change the thought of being a victim of my disease. In reality, my diagnosis gave me my life back.

At fifty-six years old and having endured a significant amount of past trauma, I wholeheartedly accept every aspect of my life and fully understand my identity today. My name is Annmarie, and I proudly serve as a Rheumatoid Arthritis Coach, as well as fulfilling roles as a wife, mother, grandma, daughter in law, sister, and friend. I am also a fierce warrior in the face of arthritis. Despite the judgements imposed upon me by others, I have discovered a profound love and acceptance for myself, regardless of the hardships I have faced. I have dedicated myself to working on personal growth and conquering my inner struggles, with the ultimate goal of stopping generational trauma.

With an unwavering sense of self-compassion, grace, consistency, and faith, I strive to create the life I desire and leave behind a legacy of resilience, strength, and empowerment. I acknowledge that I am imperfectly imperfect, and I firmly believe that pain can only overpower us if we grant it power. This realization has allowed me to embrace pain as an opportunity for personal growth, paving the way to discover my true purpose in life and provide a roadmap for others to learn from. My own roller-coaster journey has taught me valuable lessons that I now share with others, inspiring them to navigate their own paths and overcome adversity.

ABOUT THE AUTHOR

Annmarie Entner is a certified life coach who specializes in working with women who have rheumatoid arthritis. Having personal experience with this condition, Annmarie is passionate about empowering and supporting individuals on their journey of self-discovery and personal growth. She believes in embracing pain as a catalyst for personal development and sees challenges as stepping stones towards defining one's path in life.

Outside of her career as a life coach, Annmarie is a loving mother, devoted wife, and proud grandmother. She values family and finds joy in nurturing relationships and creating lasting memories with loved ones. With her compassionate and empathetic approach, Annmarie helps her clients let go of what has held them back and paves the way for positive transformation and renewed mental fitness.

Breaking the Silence

If you're looking for guidance, support, and a partner in your personal development journey, Annmarie Entner is a trusted ally. Her expertise as a certified life coach, coupled with her experience with rheumatoid arthritis and a survivor of trauma, makes her well-equipped to help you overcome obstacles and achieve a fulfilling life.

Webpage: LifeCoachingForChange.com
Instagram: ra_warrior.advocate
Facebook: Annmarie Entner

CHAPTER 13

LIFE AFTER DEATH

Barry Rothstein

In 1981, I took part in what was a union-endorsed strike for safety while working as an air traffic controller. I, along with the thousands of others on the picket lines, were fired by then President Ronald Reagan. It took me awhile to find my next career move. As the media director, it was Bill who interviewed me for a position at Sotheby's in-house advertising agency in Manhattan. As I approached his desk, I saw a good-looking, thin, bearded young man professionally dressed with piercing eyes and a quiet demeanor waiting for me.

It was 1982 and by the end of that first year working side by side, we initially became friends and then a couple. It was his wish to leave New York City to be further away from his mother and her intense mood swings and family tensions. I learned early on that Mom could be oh-so-terrific and then turn into a terror. Bill's childhood was a difficult one with severe beatings and a constant fear of his mother. I wasn't aware at that time that he also had many other innate fears that haunted him throughout his life. We decided to move to Atlanta.

We had a pretty good relationship for twenty-four years, although it was marred by his mood swings and fears that kept him constantly stressed and self-medicating with vodka. I didn't realize the intensity of his issues until much later. He had a tremendous fear of doctors that would keep him from ever going to one. He was petrified of heights. He had anxiety meeting people and dealing with others. Yet he was also very caring and friendly around the people he did get to know. He was so well-loved. Most people didn't realize that the bottles of water that he carried were usually filled with a strong vodka mix.

After five years in Atlanta and after one ice storm too many, we then moved to St. Petersburg, Florida in 1989. Bill decided to leave the corporate world of advertising as the excellent media director he had been. He decided he could no longer deal with the pressures of the advertising world. He started a cleaning business. He also became a freelance writer and photographer, and an excellent one at that. His articles, stories, and photos were periodically published in the *New York Times, St. Petersburg Times, Delta Sky, Tampa Bay Magazine* and *Watermark*, among others. We also started a successful collectibles and antique toy business that he ran.

In 2006, at Bill's insistence, we got married in Canada. Life was good and yet challenged by his mood changes and bad temperament that typically only surfaced at home or when we were alone. There were times during arguments that he punched at me and aggressively pushed me against walls and doors. This was a big contributing factor when, in early 2008, after my diagnosis of malignant melanoma, I realized life was short with no guarantees and I needed to make some changes. I tried to get Bill to go for therapy, but he refused. I couldn't deal with his mood swings any longer. I began rethinking our relationship and started to discuss separating.

That was the beginning of Bill spiraling into a depression that was truly difficult. I again tried to get him to go to a therapist, and he did go for one session. He never went back, nor did he try to find another one.

It was 2008 and the height of the recession. The collectibles business was faltering and took a nosedive. Bill's depression became worse. He stopped communicating with many of our friends. He refused to go out and socialize even with the people he cared about and those who cared about him. He only talked with his sister who lived in New Jersey and an online friend, Matt, who lived in Massachusetts.

We were a few months into our trial separation, even though we were living together. I tried getting him connected with some of my business contacts so that he could find a job beyond his sporadic writing assignments and the collectibles business that would give him more stability. We were still together, but I believe his anxiety sent him into a further downward spiral. I tried my best to encourage him and help him while trying to end our co-dependency.

Breaking the Silence

On the morning of August 3, 2008, we went our separate ways searching for items to purchase for resale. I noticed when he left that he seemed to be especially down and quiet.

I was president of The Tampa Bay Bears, a social organization that we started and ran for eight years. We had upwards of two hundred and fifty members and that Sunday was our monthly 4 p.m. meeting at Georgie's Alibi. Bill refused to go to the meetings once we started discussing separation. I went to Georgie's alone to run the proceedings. I parked the car and decided to call Bill to see how he was and what treasures he might have found at the garage sales. The conversation was brief and awkward. I knew something was very wrong. "Barry, I will always love you," Bill said as we hung up. He sounded ominous and strange. I tried contacting both his sister and Matt to see if they could contact him and check on him. No answer. My voicemail to each was brief but urgent.

"It's Barry, if you get this message, please reach out to Bill ASAP. I sense something is very wrong. I'm heading home now."

My intuition told me I needed to get back to the house immediately. I wanted to make sure he was okay. I dropped off all my paraphernalia for the meeting, got back in the car, and rushed back home ... just 1ten minutes away.

As I opened the front door I could see Bill sitting on the floor of the TV room beyond the foyer and living room. He saw me and quickly proceeded to push something under the area rug in front of him. I walked up to where he was sitting. He had a dazed look on his face. I bent down and pulled back the rug to discover a gun. We did not have a gun. My first thought was to grab it, but he reached out and got it before I could. "Please give me the gun, Bill, please," I pleaded. He obviously had been drinking. What I didn't know is that he had also taken prescription pills that his sister sent him thinking they would help him through his anxiety.

My mind was racing. I thought he could shoot me. In a panicked state, I dialed 911 not knowing what else to do. He saw me with my phone in my hand, my earbud in my ear, punching in the digits and asked, "Who are you calling? Hang up or I will do it right now." So I disconnected from the attempted call, not realizing

Breaking the Silence

that the connection had already been made. They called right back. My phone started blasting Diana Ross' "The Boss," my ringtone at the time. This song is a very upbeat, happy dance song; it made for a very jarring sound in light of the situation.

    I accidentally connected the call, but didn't talk. In my ear I heard, "Is everything okay? Is everything okay?" from the 911 dispatcher. I was facing Bill and beginning to slowly walk backwards away from him. He looked puzzled and out of sorts. As I passed the coffee table on my right in the living room, still facing him, I saw the note, "YOU KILLED ME" laying on top. In the next seconds, as I stood looking at him with his dazed expression and listening to the dispatcher on the other end of the phone, he did it.

    The gun went off and he fell forward with his head in a pool of blood. I became hysterical and ran from the house screaming and crying. We lived on a very quiet street and luckily knew and befriended many of the neighbors. A Pinellas County sheriff lived across the street and he and his brother came running when they saw me hysterically crying and standing outside. Next, my good friends and neighbors Kelly and Brandon arrived. I learned their young daughter was taking a walk down the street and heard the loud "BANG," then saw me running outside screaming. She went quickly home to tell her parents.

    I remained outside in hysterics and made a few calls to my brother and some friends. As I stood there, the police arrived and went into the house, marking it as a crime scene. One policeman remained outside with me asking interrogation questions. As far as the police were concerned, I was in the clear. But was I? I felt guilty and began to blame myself, even though I never touched the gun.

    I answered their questions and informed the police officer that we were a married couple, together over twenty-four years. That didn't seem to matter. Our marriage was still not recognized in our own country. I was treated as a suspect and a stranger. They basically discounted me as Bill's family and told me any personal items that I wanted would be sent to his sister in New Jersey, and I would need to deal with her for their return. Being treated like a stranger to Bill and not the husband I was made things more traumatic and unsettling.

I remained outside with the police and the special homicide/death unit reliving what occurred in front of my eyes. A few more friends arrived and joined Kelly, Brandon and me in front of my house. Two of them decided to take me away from the scene once I was told I could leave. Of course I was concerned for Belle and Maurice, our cats, but it seemed like the right thing to do. My two friends went into the house, packed a bag for me, and we left for their home not too far away. I couldn't have asked for better support from those that surrounded me at my most vulnerable time.

It was Kelly and Brandon who were instrumental in the initial clean up so that we could eventually enter the home free of blood and broken glass from the big screen TV that was also hit by the blast of the gun. The thought of reentering the house for the first time terrified me. My mind continued to work overtime reliving the moments and blaming myself for Bill's death. The shock and horror of what I witnessed sent me into a hysterical state of emotions. I was crying constantly wherever I went.

At this point I needed to get back into the house if only for our cats. It had been about two weeks of me staying away. I had to gather my strength to return. I also had to begin thinking about the process of what needed to be done in planning for Bill's funeral and service. My mental state made it difficult for me to think clearly, but there were things that needed my attention and had to get done.

Bill's funeral was planned by me, along with Brandon and Kelly. Their support and assistance helped me make sensible choices regarding the memorial.

The arrangements were set. Bill's sister would be arriving and staying with me at the house. A few close friends also flew down. My doctor had prescribed medication for me to stay calm and centered. It helped some. The early evening service and memorial was witnessed by what seemed like hundreds of people––friends, relatives, business acquaintances, and peers.

Breaking the Silence

It wasn't until months later when I sat down that I was able to read page after page of the guest roster to comprehend just how many people had been there. I couldn't work even though I had deadlines pending. Although my bosses and the staff at work were extremely understanding and patient, I knew my job was critical for the magazine's continued success. I needed a break and went to visit a friend in New York. During that time my friends in St. Petersburg took care of the cats and arranged for the floor to be replaced. I truly don't know what I would have done without the support and help of these few friends that came to my rescue.

I remained in New York for a week. I was emotionally drained and still cried hysterically throughout the day and night. I was feeling guilty while also telling myself that couples of all types and ages separate and marriages of all lengths end in divorce, and yet they get through it usually without someone committing suicide.

I had to face my life as a survivor and go back home to Belle and Maurice and the memories that would never go away. It was 2008, and the height of the recession. It dawned on me that I was stuck in my house unless I wanted to give it away. Home prices were at their lowest. So there I was trying to go back to work, returning each evening to our cats and the house that now would not let me forget even for a second what had taken place weeks before. My thoughts of guilt continued. Every time I turned the key and opened the door flashbacks streamed through my mind reliving the terror and horror of Bill's death.

I was referred to a therapist and started seeing him regularly. That continued for three years. I could be found hysterically crying in the supermarket or at work or on the street corner, which led to my doctor prescribing antidepressants. I took those pills for a full year. I suffered and continue to suffer from PTSD. Loud noises, fireworks, seeing a movie or a show with shootings send me into hysterics even to this day, sixteen years later.

A few months went by, and just as I thought I was beginning to deal with it all, I started the task of going through Bill's office cleaning and getting rid of things in my attempt to clear the house of the memories and the constant reminders of his death. It was then that I came upon the letter Bill wrote addressed to me in his excellent writing style that he intentionally and carefully placed for me to find at a later date. I only remember how hostile and hateful the letter was. It was cruel and meant to create havoc within me ... and havoc and distress it certainly did cause. I was hysterical once again. I had to remember that the letter was written by someone not in his own mind. I called my therapist, crying. At the wise suggestion of Dr. Davich, I destroyed the letter and continued the job of clearing the house of his papers and things that I could no longer hold on to without it affecting me. Blaming myself was indeed my first reaction. The guilt I felt was normal, but I was not to blame, nor was Bill.

Dr. Davich explained it to me in layman's terms: "The brain is hard-wired for self-preservation. It's a firewall, if you may, to keep one from self-harm and even attacks from others. However, when someone has a depression so severe as Bill's was, it gives them the capability of breaking through that firewall. His breakthrough had to have happened days earlier giving him the ability to plan and then execute his death including the purchase of the gun. He was in an altered state. And you or anyone else, would not have been able to pull him out of it. You need to learn to give yourself forgiveness and know there was nothing you could have done."

I came to understand that I was not at fault. Emotionally I was struggling to accept that and forgive myself for not seeing this coming and not being able to stop him. Neither of us was to blame—not me and not Bill. Yes, I became angry that he did this to himself, to me, to his family and to his friends. And yet I also understand that his mental state was not the Bill we all loved and cared about was not the same Bill who pulled the trigger.

In the months that followed, my mental state was foggy. The antidepressants made it worse, but at least they did hold back some of the tears. Many who I had thought of as friends vanished from sight never to be heard from again. I had to learn through therapy that people run from tragedy, especially suicide. People just don't know how to deal with it and feel better ignoring it and not speaking about it.

There was also the melodrama I heard about through others that many in our circle of friends and club members were actually blaming me for Bill's death. I knew to dismiss those thoughts.

There are too many suicides in America each year. Talking about it and stopping the fear of discussing it can help. It helps those who are thinking about doing it and it helps survivors deal with their ongoing grief and emotional distress.

Life goes on, as they say. I deal with the aftermath of Bill's suicide daily. There is no telling what will trigger me to start crying. I can be at the theatre watching a show or movie that involves guns, shootings, or loud noises. I can be listening to my music when a certain song comes on. I can be home on New Year's Eve or the Fourth of July and become hysterical when the neighborhood fireworks are exploding. I can hear of another person dealing with suicide. The list goes on and on, and the emotions are still there and raw, but it's important to face it all and move on.

I am remarried, now going on six years, and I am with someone who understands my need to deal with the suicide. I will be dealing with it for the rest of my life. In the meantime, I don't wish anyone else to go through the special kind of grief and mental despair caused by suicide. When I speak to people about what happened most times they respond with, "I can't imagine." All I can say to them is, "You don't want to."

Besides making a conscious effort to talk about it, my husband and I do the "American Federation for Suicide Prevention Out of the Darkness" walk each year and raise funds in the hopes of helping those contemplating suicide and the survivors of suicide. The walk usually takes place in St. Petersburg annually, sometime in the fall. We are always looking for others to join us and be a part of Team Billy.

There are many great organizations out there to offer help when its most needed. I have learned to talk about Bill's death and his suicide to keep it in people's minds. Suicides happen every day and my hope is that my story will be an inspiration for even one person contemplating it, and just maybe, help them realize what their act could do to those left behind. It's okay to reach out for help. I hope the survivors reading my story will understand that there is no place for blame or guilt and come to realize there is life and happiness for all of us after. There is life after death.

ABOUT THE AUTHOR

  Barry Rothstein has made St. Petersburg, Florida his home for the past thirty-five years. Originally from New York City, Rothstein has had a varied career and life having been an air traffic controller at the New York Enroute Traffic Control Center, a marketing account executive, a telecom business-to-business account executive, and currently a realtor in the Tampa Bay region.
  Throughout his life, art has played an important role with his rich background in drawing, illustration, and for the last twenty-five years as an accomplished pastel artist. He was accepted into the Pastel Society of America over a decade ago. As Rothstein recounts, "Since I could pick up a crayon, art is and has always been a constant in my life bringing comfort when times looked their bleakest and taking my mind off things that have caused pain. Most importantly it ultimately has brought much joy to myself and others."
  Through his art, Rothstein showcases his power of determination and resilience. Rothstein's success as a color blind artist serves as an inspiration to many aspiring artists and those who may face their own obstacles in pursuing their passion in life. He reminds us that we all can flourish even in the face of adversity.
  Rothstein loves to stay busy whether it is helping people find their forever home or creating a commissioned pastel painting for others. Rothstein resides with his husband and their three cat fur babies.

You can reach Rothstein and see his work through his websites:

www.artbyrothstein.com
www.barryrothstein.com

Breaking the Silence

HERE ARE SOME SUICIDE PREVENTION ORGANIZATIONS AND RESOURCES:

988 Suicide and Crisis Lifeline 24 hours
AFSP (American Federation for Suicide Prevention)
https://afsp.org/findsupport/resources/

NIMH (National Institute of Mental Health)
https://www.nimh.nih.gov/health/topics/suicideprevention/index.shtml

SPTS (Society for the Prevention of Teen Suicide)
http://www.sptsusa.org/

SPRC (Suicide Prevention Resource Center)
http://www.sprc.org/

Crisis Line 1-800-273-TALK (8255)

Crisis Text Line
http://www.crisistextline.org/

The Trevor Project
www.thetrevorproject.org/ - Leading national organization providing crisis intervention and suicide prevention services to LGBTQ+ young people under twenty-five

CHAPTER 14

THE WARRIOR WITHIN

Beverly Hatfield

Please embark on a journey with me that may sometimes feel like an emotional roller coaster. But if one can look past the horrors, there is a beautiful tenacity displayed throughout. This chapter combines elements of hardship and resilience, woven together like the patches of a quilt, bound by faith and inner strength.

My earliest memory doesn't involve my mother's warm smile or the playful moments with my steadfast older brother. Instead, it is etched with the memory of being led upstairs by my babysitter's husband. At the time, I was a spirited, green-eyed young girl with bronze hair, not yet six years old, residing in Salina, Kansas. Kindergarten had just commenced, necessitating my attendance at the babysitter's home after school, given its half-day schedule. The new sitter, located down the street, was married with two boys. Little did I know what awaited me, despite assurances that it would be "fun."

Everything was fine until it wasn't.

I opened my eyes to my babysitter's husband looming over me. Confusion swept over me. Where was the babysitter? She was there when I laid down for my nap. He took me by my hand and guided me toward the stairs, leading me up to the room at the top. This was my very first memory and my first rape. Let me introduce you to Perpetrator No. 1. The assaults persisted every time my babysitter left me asleep under his care.

Desperate to confide in my mom, I would scream and threaten him that I would reveal the truth. Yet, each time, he would silence me with a chilling reminder: if I spoke up, he would invade our home and kill my entire family. Paralyzed by fear, I couldn't speak the truth. I couldn't put them in danger. My only option was to remain silent to shield my loved ones from harm. What a monumental responsibility for a young girl.

Breaking the Silence

Several years passed, I reached the age of eight or nine, and my mom, brother, and I had relocated to Colorado Springs. It marked my fourth school change in just four years. Despite the frequent moves, I found solace in anticipating the upcoming school year. My older sister, seventeen years my senior, was now living in Colorado Springs and I was excited that her new stepson would join my class, bringing a sense of familiarity to an otherwise unfamiliar environment. For the first time since our moves began, I felt a sense of excitement and security.

Everything was fine until it wasn't.

I remember standing in line at the teacher's desk to ask questions or submit a paper. Waiting in line at the teacher's desk was a routine part of my daily experience. I hated standing in line at the teacher's desk, and as I recollect these memories, I have a guttural feeling of waiting patiently to go to slaughter. The act of standing in line was not outwardly violent, but the pain and destruction these moments have imprinted upon me to this day are profound. Sometimes, when I had a question, I had to engage in a game called "handcuffs" to be released back to my desk. That was the form of payment that was required. Handcuffs entailed sitting on his chair with my hands behind my back and my hands touching his crotch. Let me formally introduce you to Perpetrator No. 2, my third-grade teacher.

All the other teachers and students appeared to adore him. Our class would get candy bars and regular movie screenings as "treats." Mr. C was cool, they said. The excitement was palpable on movie day in the classroom. I hated movie day. We'd arrange ourselves on the floor in front of the wheeled TV. The lights dimmed, and the blinds were drawn shut. Mr. C. would lie on the floor with all the students and candy bars were given out during movie time. I never knew when it was my turn to get a candy bar, but when I did, it always came with a price. He would put his hand down my pants, or he would put my hand down his pants when the lights were off; this was the payment for the candy bar. He had on plastic underwear. Yes, you read that correctly: plastic. Over forty years later, I still have difficulty wrapping my brain around that

Breaking the Silence

fact. The understanding that everything came with a price became permanently etched in my mind.

My friend and I, accompanied by her brother, would walk through our trailer park after school. During these walks, we would talk about what he had done to us that day, but I never shared these experiences outside of those walks home.

Several months later, my mom came to me and asked if my teacher had touched me. I said yes. I discovered that my friend's brother had overheard our conversations and confided in his mother about what was happening to the girls in Mr. C's class. She then reached out to my mom to inform her what had happened. Thank you, brother (and to all those who speak up for those who cannot), for speaking up when I could not.

My mom wasted no time in heading to the school to address the situation with the principal, only to encounter resistance. All beloved Mr. C; how could he possibly be involved? After all, he boasted thirty-two years of teaching experience, and this was the first of such complaints. Even my cousin, who shared the same classroom, turned against me, branding me a liar. Throughout this ordeal, I remained steadfast in my truth, but the isolation was overwhelming. Parents of kids in other classes were not allowed to play with me, and I lost most of my friends, other than a few girls from my class. At school, both students and staff treated me differently, yet I was not removed from his class. I had to endure every day looking at my perpetrator.

One day, while on the playground, I sought help from a female teacher when my zipper broke. My mother had already reported my teacher to the principal, but instead of the female assisting me herself, she escorted me inside to Mr. C. The inside of the school was hushed, with everyone being outside for recess. I was scared. He expressed gratitude to the female teacher for bringing me in to seek help. She smiled and walked off, leaving me with a very real monster. Internally, I was screaming. I desperately did not want to be left alone with him. This action resulted in another occurrence of betrayal. I took what was done to me and again, didn't say a word.

Breaking the Silence

Eventually, my mother moved us back to Kansas to get away from the torment. I remember driving in our truck, packed with everything we owned, as we crossed states to safety. But I didn't feel safe. As I sat in the back seat, I had terrors, thinking he was on the bumper coming to get me as we drove. I couldn't voice my fears because my mom was moving me from the terror, yet she didn't know the terror that went on in my mind every single day of my life.

I would have to return to Colorado Springs several more times over that year for court appearances. In the end, Perpetrator No. 2 escaped without consequences, while the principal received a minor penalty of a $200 fine for failure to report. This reinforced the notion that the truth held little weight. People believed what aligned with their desires. It also highlighted the unfortunate reality that men could act with impunity towards me without facing any repercussions. This experience also taught me to always move on with life and not discuss what happened.

My mother was my strongest advocate in seeking justice. However, her reluctance to discuss what happened added to the pain I was already experiencing. In my upbringing, discussions about emotions and feelings were rare. The prevailing message was to toughen up and move forward with life. I am deeply convinced that my mother loved me with all her heart, and I understand that she, too, carried her own trauma from what happened to me. My mother's primary responsibility was to ensure my safety, and when she placed her trust in those in authority, only to have that trust betrayed, it must have caused her immense pain to know she had failed. My mom is no longer on this earthly plane, but I know in my heart of hearts that she did the best she could at that time, and I am grateful and blessed to have had her as my mom.

Life moved forward. At the age of thirteen, I resided in Clearwater, Florida, attending the sixth grade. I had to miss school on Fridays to drive to Ruskin with my mom to harvest vegetables at the local farms, ensuring we had products to sell at the flea market that weekend. One afternoon, on our way home, after seven years of agonizing silence, I finally confided in my mom about

Breaking the Silence

Perpetrator No. 1. The conversation was short. My mom reassured me that I didn't need to worry about him hurting anyone else because he was in prison for raping little boys. We never talked about it again.

At the age of fifteen, I resided in Cocoa, Florida. I was a freshman in high school, living in an apartment complex with my mom and brother. I was restricted to staying within the gates of the community, as it was considered safe within the confines of the complex. We lived across the street from the local community college, and many college students lived in my complex. One day, as I was walking past the office, a white Mustang GT with an out-of-state license plate drove by. It parked directly ahead of me, and a handsome, blond-haired, well-built male stepped out of the car wearing a football jersey from the local college. This boy was incredibly handsome, and he showed interest in me. At eighteen, he was in Florida on a football scholarship. He treated me kindly, and we enjoyed watching TV and having conversations together. Sometimes, he would even pick me up from school and drive me home. I met my first real boyfriend. I was an inexperienced girl, naive when it came to boys, but I felt safe with him.

Everything was fine until it wasn't.

We watched some sitcoms on TV, and we kissed on the couch. He moved his hand between my legs, and I said, "No, I don't want to." He tried several more times, with each attempt encountering my defiance, until his patience ran out, and he ripped my jeans off and did what he wanted to with my body. I cried. I was scared, and fear rendered my body immobile, locking me in place as if I had turned to stone. Let me introduce you to Perpetrator No. 3.

After he had his way with my body, I scraped myself up and walked home. I walked into the house and never said a word to anyone. I didn't tell my mom, I didn't tell my brother. I didn't have my own bedroom, as I had to share the bedroom with my mom. I went directly to the bathroom to shower and cry. It was my fault, I told myself. I shouldn't have been alone in his home. I shouldn't have kissed him; that permitted him to do whatever he wanted to. Those are the stories I told myself for years.

Breaking the Silence

At eighteen, I resided with someone I had once considered a friend in Abilene, Kansas. Despite being in high school, I worked full-time to cover my share of the bills. It posed its challenges, but that's just the way life goes. It's all about confronting adversity head-on and pushing forward.

Everything was fine until it wasn't.

One evening, my roommate's boyfriend paid a visit, accompanied by his friend, whom I recognized. I had been on a date with him before, but I had declined further invitations for additional dates as I didn't feel it was a suitable match. I felt extremely uneasy about his visit and expressed my concerns to my roommate. She reassured me, saying, "It's okay, you're overreacting." We all were watching TV in the living room, and eventually, my roommate and her boyfriend left to go into her bedroom. I quickly moved to the other side of the couch, attempting to create as much distance as possible from him. However, he disregarded my boundaries and assaulted me on the couch.

He told me I deserved this for believing I was better than him. I cried out for help from my roommate, but unfortunately, assistance never arrived. Meet Perpetrator No. 4. When she finally came out of the room, I was curled into a tight ball on the couch, seeking solace in my familiar embrace. He left with my roommate's boyfriend, acting as if nothing had happened. I remember crying and asking why she didn't help me, to which she responded, "I thought you were joking." Huh? Who jokes about something like that? At that moment, I came to the stark realization: I was navigating this world alone, with only myself to shield me from harm.

A couple of months later, my roommate held a going away party for me as I was heading back to Florida to be near my mom and brother. During this party, Perpetrator No. 4 walked into my house. He and his accompanying friends negated my very loud yells for this rapist to leave my house, yet he continued to prance around my home as if I wasn't screaming in the background. Everyone at that party was going to know what he did to me. I began to see red; I grabbed an empty vodka bottle and went to hit him over the head. Thank goodness all the stars aligned, and someone saw what I was doing and bumped my hand. Instead of breaking the bottle across his head, it crashed on the door jam above. I don't remember who saved me that day, but I am so grateful in this moment they did. If I had hit him, I would have gone to jail. If I had hurt him, that would have changed me. At the time, I was angry. I was angry that someone would help him and not me, but as I type these words, that is not my experience. They *did* help me, I just couldn't see it at the time.

It was June 8. I was twenty-eight years old and a single mother of two boys living in Kansas. The second Thursday of June was the kickoff for the yearly festival, and the excitement was palpable throughout the town. I was so excited about my lunch date on this fateful afternoon. The lunch date went well, and we attended opening night concerts at the festival that evening. It was all a whirlwind, meeting each other's family and friends on our first date.

Reflecting on the past, I now recognize the warning signs that were present from the very beginning. However, my focus was solely on my goal: to discover a man who could serve as a wonderful father figure for my sons. By the time July came around, he was living in my apartment with the boys and me. Three months in, I was begging him to go to counseling. He was an alcoholic, controlling, and a miserable human being to be around, but he accepted my boys and me. I couldn't leave; who else would date a single mother with no education and who had two boys under seven? "It's not that bad, at least we are not being physically abused," I told myself. I told myself that I would protect my boys and take the brunt of his discourse, and my boys wouldn't be affected. I was so very wrong; my boys were dramatically affected.

We bought our first house together within that first year. I moved around my entire life. I had never had a home to call my own before. My boys went to good schools, and everything I had envisioned for them was coming to fruition. Life was good, I thought.

Everything was fine until it wasn't.

Breaking the Silence

The boys were in bed, and I had cleaned up from the day and had just started to get ready for bed. My ex came upstairs intoxicated after watching a Lakers basketball game. This was not an unusual state for him. This evening, he wanted sexy time, and I was honestly disgusted by his intoxication and refused his advances. Such behavior was utterly unacceptable, I soon found out. Consequently, I found myself forcefully pushed onto the bed, with my legs dangling over the edge. He climbed on top of me, took what he wanted, and passed out on top of me.

I couldn't breathe; his dead weight was crushing me. I laid there, screaming inside for him to get off, but I was terrified to wake him up. Meet my most prolific offender, my ex, Perpetrator No. 5. I endured many violations during my ten years with him, so many that I even coined a term when he would do with my body as he chose; I called it "gas stationing." This was when I came to understand that normalized rape within a relationship was a very real thing.

By the time I left, I was thirty-nine years old and had suffered countless violations over thirty-three years. For years, I carried the weight of self-blame, questioning what I could have done differently to prevent multiple men from violating me. I have concluded that the need to change lies not within myself but within societal norms. We must address the acceptance of such behaviors and the tendency to shift the blame on the victim rather than acknowledging the systemic issues at play. Another realization I've come to during this journey is the significance of intentional listening. As parents, we often claim to listen yet fail to hear what others convey. Moreover, we may overlook the impact of our responses. When faced with uncertainty about how to respond, it's crucial to address and discuss the matter rather than ignore it, no matter how complex or hard the subject matter is to talk about.

Society often dictates that once a traumatic event concludes, we should swiftly move on from it. However, the reality is far more complex, as numerous factors influence our individual experiences. Our past interactions, coupled with our interpretations of them, intensify the impact of trauma, making it difficult to move on easily. Unresolved traumatic experiences manifest in various harmful ways, including illness, addiction, risky behaviors, self-loathing, and animosity toward others, none of which benefit us in any manner. Healing those pains is imperative to finding peace.

Since 2011, my journey has consisted of self-recovery, embracing self-love, and fostering acceptance. This self-love journey has proven to be one of the toughest challenges I've faced, yet it's also been the most rewarding and fulfilling experience of my life. After fifty-one years of experiences shaping my narrative, I now sit here, pen in hand, engulfed by the self-discovery and revelations that have come with choosing to unveil my truth. I always knew I would be an author; little did I know my first writing endeavor would be to unlock the taboo topic of sexual assault and my very real experiences.

Today I am focused on unfolding my experiences for others to learn from. We all experience hardships in life, a truth we cannot escape. What can be changed is how we respond to any given hardship. I have come to understand that enduring hardships without experiencing growth is akin to enduring hell on earth. For many years of my life, my power was stripped away from me. But now I've discovered how to reclaim that power by refusing to let hardships control my future, unleashing my strength once again.

What is my superpower, you ask? It's love. I love all humankind, but first and foremost, I love myself. I embrace all versions of myself. While I may not consistently execute flawlessly, I am flawless in my creation and always authentically me. I have learned to harness the pain and create a magical perspective with insights that serve my highest good. Continuously evolving, I explore the depths of myself, realizing the profound love and light within me that can uplift and inspire others. Spreading this enlightenment to those unaware enriches me greatly. I embrace the divinity within me daily, radiating love and light to every corner, bridging all seven degrees of separation. This is my path. This is my calling.

ABOUT THE AUTHOR

Beverly M. Hatfield is a compassionate author dedicated to sharing her stories of healing and resilience to spur a movement to encourage others to speak and live in their truths. With thirty-three years of experience in health care, she has dedicated nineteen years as a registered nurse working with fragile populations such as neonatal intensive care, pediatrics, hospice, and as a sexual assault nurse examiner. She is an intentional wellness coach, trauma coach, and shamanic reiki and spiritual hypnotherapy practitioner. She focuses on mental health advocacy and support leveraging her extensive background to empower individuals towards holistic wellness. Beverly weaves together a tapestry of true experiences, offering a glimpse into the transformative power of overcoming trauma and invites others to embark on a journey of healing and hope.

https://www.nursebeverly.com/

CHAPTER 15

UNHEARD SCREAMS:

EMPLOYEES BATTLING TRAUMA IN THE WORKPLACE

Lisa J. Crawford

In the hushed corridors of corporate offices and the bustling environments of modern workplaces, countless stories of struggle and resilience go untold. Behind the masks of professional decorum and productivity lies a darker reality that many employees face daily: workplace trauma. The mask we wear at work can sometimes be debilitating to our mental and physical well-being.

I have experienced the silent battles fought in conference rooms and cubicles, where the pressures of deadlines, the weight of unrealistic expectations, and the shadows of bullying and harassment take a toll on individuals. In a world where professional success is often prioritized over personal well-being, it's time to acknowledge the unseen wounds and to champion a culture of empathy and support.

When I grew up, I was taught to help others. In my home I saw my mother, sister, and brother give to those without food, shelter, clothing. I remember being amazed that they did not know the people, but when you see the action daily it becomes a part of your soul. I remember my first job was as a hostess at Red Lobster and I adored the smiles that people gave when I simply sat them and gave them a menu. I loved that feeling so much. I continued on to work as an after-school teacher for the YMCA, then an aid to those that were disabled; all of my jobs have been in service. When I finally reached the hospitality industry, it was the perfect match for my personality.

In 2004, I started my hospitality career in a four-diamond hotel. I was full of hope and happiness as a concierge. To be excited to go to work was not just a thought for me, it was simply a way of life. My heart is that of a servant, and in the hospitality industry there must be an internal need to serve and make others feel welcomed in the hotel. One thing that I was so proud of about my character was that I never had to fake being a good person and a happy employee to my guests or my coworkers. Hospitality is in my DNA.

As I stated, I started out as a concierge, "Ms. Fix It." I loved it. I adored creating relationships with the guests and companies that stopped by my desk for information. Being able to help someone in need because they did not have time or simply did not want to plan was exhilarating. I was tipped so well it was like a second job. Three years flew by, and I was promoted to a catering assistant, and I loved it. Most of all I adored my catering director; she was amazing and brought out the best of me by believing in me to take her clients and tour them and get their information. She made sure I had my own business cards, and can you believe this, she had to fight for me to get them since in the higher ups' eyes I was just an assistant. She treated me according to her faith in me and the skills that I possessed. During that time with her, I realized that I was selling her clients on the property and all she had to do was the contract. It was a wonderful feeling.

After a while, a different leader came into my life, and she taught me that leaders can acknowledge when they are wrong and change. I appreciated her so much for that lesson. She was supportive and so helpful to me as I continued to grow. Then her life shifted, and she told me I had to do the unthinkable: go into the sales department with a leader that did not like me at all. Can you remember a time when you found out some information and it felt like Mike Tyson had gut punched you and there was no return from the pain? Well, this is what that conversation felt like in my heart. I felt this way because I saw how this leader treated their staff for over three years, and I did not want one second of that department.

As soon as I got into the department, I immediately felt the pressure and disdain for my very presence. I talked with the scared part of me to understand that I deserved to be in the department simply because I loved people and wanted to see them have a great experience in my hotel. I knew that I could sell to anyone with

Breaking the Silence

breath in their body. That was a win for my need to serve and for the bottom line for the hotel, so I made that my focus!

This leader made me feel like I was invisible. When I was spoken to, it was harsh and condescending. We had a meeting every Monday and I noticed that this leader never looked at me when he was speaking or trying to train. My problem was that I was never intentionally trained. After my first month or so, I felt so many screaming negative emotions about being in the department. For the first time I acknowledged that I was truly sad within myself. When you are a person that is filled with love and care, it is hard to have a leader that pulls a tiny piece of your soul out every day. I took that pain home silently with me daily.

As an employee, I wanted someone to hear me when I spoke about this leader, but no one heard me. It was like they were untouchable because of their skills and ability to produce, and that is what every hotel wants, right? Even at the expense of the mental health of those that reported to this leader. The mask that I wore in my life during this time was suffocating my very soul and my body was physically breaking down.

When we are in bad situations in life, sometimes we stay because of financial reasons or the unwillingness to leave the familiar. I stayed because I thought I belonged and unfortunately, this company was not just a job; it became my identity. That alone can be a devastating blow to self-love and self-care. How many times in life do we allow our titles to become our identity? Sometimes in the title is a mountain of stress, responsibility and we lose our true selves.

Over the next three years, I suffered the loss of my sight in both eyes. During the first sight loss, I never missed a day of work. I sat in my office with the overhead light off, a dim lamp, and sunglasses. I continued in my title and the expectations of the job. I was also in college, to receive my bachelor's degree and I could not miss a class. The second one, I recognized it a little earlier. The ophthalmologist wanted to try a freeze method in which a needle was stuck into my eye without anesthesia. I watched the needle enter my eye multiple times and was sent home in agony. The very next day I had to have emergency surgery.

Breaking the Silence

My migraines were trying to take me out. I stayed sick and sad, but I smiled every day to my clients and coworkers because they kept me afloat. Sometimes a valet had to come and get me out of my car because I was stuck in the car and couldn't move. Can you imagine being stuck in torment alone in a car with no strength of your own to open a car door? That should have been a defining moment for me, but it was not. I tried harder to be better. Once I got to my office no one knew the challenges I faced trying to get into the building that was diagonal to this building.

I am going to be very transparent; maybe there was a desperate part of me that wanted to be accepted by this leader. Did I need to prove to them that I was a good salesperson? When we went out for sales outings and there was food, drinks, and laughter, I always tried to sit by this leader. Isn't that crazy? It was the only time that we could talk and I could get to know something about them firsthand. Unfortunately, those opportunities were few and far between. One day, I went to the doctor's office because I could not stop crying in my sleep, and the doctor said, "You are depressed." I needed to be put on antidepressants. What?! "You are suffering," he said.

How can employees go through so much on the job and leaders never observe that there may be a problem? This team only had about six sales managers so why didn't the leader see me? I even passed out twice on my way to a one-on-one from the anxiety of listening to the belittling and condescending leader. Both times when I opened my eyes, they were the one over me trying to assist. That was interesting to see that the very one that I had allowed to emotionally drain me was the first one I saw when my eyes opened.

So many things happened after that, but I had to go to God in prayer and seek divine help. He allowed my four-year-old granddaughter to say, "Granny, what did the leader do to you today?" She said the entire name. I knew at that moment I allowed someone to take over everything about me. It was time for a change. I did not leave my job, but I changed my perspective and my responses to this person. It was so hard to just be in my own skin, but I had kids and grandkids to take care of. I was also a minister during this time and a student. Talk about pressure all the way around, but I was determined to prove to myself that I was worthy, and I would fight the good fight. When we fight the good fight, is it really good for the soul? It was not while I was going through it, but I think I will chalk it up to stubbornness.

I achieved the highest accomplishment that I could by becoming a "platinum" sales manager at 17 percent above my goal. I thought I had really done something great, but two months before I was to go to the sales conference to be one of the few Black women to walk that stage, I was let go! I didn't even cry or show a drop of emotion during that meeting. I had lost so much of myself that it was as if I was numb, hurt, and happy all rolled up into one ball of silent confusion.

Sometimes if you don't move, God will move you. This leader did not order my award for me. It is so funny to me now, but at the time I was in amazement and a little lost. What the devil meant for evil, God meant for my good. I wrote and published a book, got evicted by the sheriff, lost my car, and had to live in so many hotels over the next twenty-four days. While I was in eviction court there was a woman that came over to me and asked what I was doing there. I told her that I was getting evicted like everyone else. She asked if I had a housing program certificate. I did not but I told her that I think my daughter did, though she could not find an apartment. She gave me her card and I forwarded it to my daughter, and she was able to get an apartment through this lady. I met a man online who introduced me to a company that needed reps to lease apartments, and they loved hospitality people. I moved away and every location had to provide me with an apartment and a vehicle. Then I ended up right back in hospitality, traveling across the United States doing what I love: being a service leader and expert sales manager.

There is a scripture (Genesis 22:13-19) in the Bible that speaks of "A ram in the bush." It refers to a story about God telling Abraham to sacrifice his son Isaac. Because of his willingness to do what was commanded God provided a ram in the bush to sacrifice. In my case, God provided me with the woman in court to solve a housing problem and the gentleman that I met to solve my employment issue. The burdens of emotional turmoil that I experienced on the job at the hands of a leader that I allowed to make me *feel* invisible and that I did not matter was replaced with the very thing that my heart desired: to serve and to travel.

No matter what happens in your life, you can make it work out for your good and be productive. I took the poor treatment I received and allowed it to become my speaking platform for employees and leaders. I take responsibility for allowing someone to take me on the roller coaster of their leadership style that was opposite of my soul.

A few things to be mindful of in the workplace:

- Silent Suffering: To find a workplace that actually cares about their employees seems to be few and far between. I have polled employees all over the United States about how they feel in their positions. So many employees stated that they simply want to be respected and heard. Any position that requires customer engagement can be a torture chamber because the customers are brutal on the phone and in person. Management does not have a moment to greet an employee by their name or ask if they are okay. Why is this? It is their job. The employee is silently suffering, waiting for their shift to be complete so that they can breathe. For most they still have to go home to a different type of stress with obligations of family, home, church, and friends. So when does the individual breathe for real?

- Toxic Environment: It is mind blowing when I see bad behaviors being overlooked and the employees that work hard are punished. This is a toxic environment. When bad behavior is not documented it opens the door for bad behaviors to run rampant in the workplace. I met a young lady that worked long hours, achieved great sales, and was a genuine soul to the co-workers and clients. Yet her managers wanted more and spoke to her so disrespectfully. I was enraged and I made it my business to praise her on a regular basis. But there was one employee that kept up so much discord on the property, was lazy, and had a bad attitude. This person was promoted to supervisor of the good employee. How is this fair? This promotion squeezed the greatness from the young lady and it broke my heart. Toxic behaviors trickle down to the undeserving.

- Mental Health Impact: I never realized how important it is to pay attention to your mental health. I was the one that stuffed my emotions and feelings into a silent box of my soul. I had to learn the hard way that suppression is not the way to solve problems or handle emotions. When you are not one with yourself within, it affects everything about you, and it shows up in your actions, tone, and conversations. Mental health in the workplace is vital for a successful workday. I have seen some take advantage of companies that offer mental health days and they come back to work just as contrary as ever. I believe that finding a space during the day to go outside and walk or look up at the sky, sit by a tree, etc. is important. Find something that you can do consistently to keep yourself grounded and productive.

- Leadership Failures: Everything rises and falls on leadership. That sounds daunting for a person in leadership unless they have integrity, truth, empathy, relationship building qualities, and knowledge of the business. Leadership is simply a title, but it is up to the person to bring it to life. This is where failure begins for some of these titled leaders. The things I have seen over the past twenty years in my industry, I am in utter disbelief how the worst leaders are praised by their superiors and those that bend over backwards to create a welcoming environment for the employees are punished by being told they do not do enough. Leadership failures trickle down from the top, and if those that catch those storms of negativity are not strong enough they will become the same or the company will lose them. If corporate sends negativity to the general manager, how much strength does it take for the general manager to not send negativity to the directors, management, supervisors, and captains? Who is left with the brunt of the wrath? That would be the employees that work for under $15 per hour. That is heartbreaking and frustrating. They are spoken to the worst, disrespected the most, and paid the least.

- Voicing Concerns: Employees want to be able to voice their concerns and truly be heard. Is this possible without consequences? I heard an employee state once that HR is for management and not for the employees. That made me so sad because I was faced with those feelings also. I went to HR several times about one leader and I was told that maybe I should seek other employment. They said it without any hesitation or thought of all of the revenue I brought to the company or how I adored my clients and coworkers. I can understand why an employee would be hesitant to speak up about unfair treatment.

- Empowerment Through Solidarity: There is strength in being on one page in the workplace. It takes a foundation creating a solid set of expectations, relationship building, true teamwork, and a desire to be the best. It has to be a team effort. Is this possible in today's workplace? One of my clients shared her love for her workplace. She stated how upper management will come by and individually chat with employees. They took time to build relationships with each employee. The company only had about a hundred employees but they were committed to letting each one know how important they were to the team. Solidarity in the workplace takes intentional actions daily.

During the time of my trauma, I felt abandoned by HR and any management above my leader. I felt that speaking about what happened would turn around and be my fault.

Breaking the Silence

I have been physically assaulted three times by men with no soul and they took from me in ways that can never be returned. When the police (HR) got involved in one of the assaults, I was asked what I did to bring this behavior to myself? Was I dressed appropriately? Was I dancing provocatively? Was I drinking? In those moments I felt that if I could not trust the police then who could I trust to give me a voice in this situation? I know that this is a dark comparison, but having had trauma prior to workplace trauma, I was triggered. Not only did I have to fight the demons of the past, but I also had to wear a mask of "I am fine" and suffer in silence.

I want to encourage everyone that reads my story to pay attention to yourself and recognize when something or someone is taking you out of character in your heart and soul. You are worthy of great things, and you are so important to the earth. Each one of you was born with a special and divine gift in your DNA. Never forget that and know that you are not alone. Trauma and triggers can change to testimonies and transformations.

ABOUT THE AUTHOR

Lisa J. Crawford, founder, author, speaker, and coach at LJC Motivations, is a well-known leader in this industry, committed to delivering impactful work. Lisa's leadership style is characterized by a blend of empathy, authenticity, and a commitment to developing a supportive and inclusive environment. She focuses on people being the best version of themselves at home and work.

With over two decades of experience as a motivational speaker, life coach, nonfiction author, and hospitality consultant, Lisa brings a wealth of expertise to her work. Under the leadership of Lisa, LJC Motivations is dedicated to enhancing individuals' well-being by providing motivation and support to help them cultivate deep self-love and commitment. The main goal is to assist people in discovering their full potential in both personal and professional aspects of their lives.

Breaking the Silence

LJC Motivations offers the following services:
- ☐ Motivational speaking
- ☐ Customized soft skills training for various departments in the hospitality industry
- ☐ Expertise in relationship-building techniques for professional and personal contexts
- ☐ Assistance with self-confidence issues related to work and personal challenges
- ☐ Consulting services in hospitality, specializing in sales and customer relationship development

"Leaders must possess the quality of humanity, treating people with dignity and respect."

CHAPTER 16

LUCKY

Rebecca Binny

    A gentle breeze softly sweeps across the Mediterranean Sea, caressing my skin as I begin to write my chapter. I'm blessed to write from a place as beautiful as this. It was just last night that my husband and I flew into Nice, one of our many getaways we run off to since we got married less than a year ago. With whatever haphazard, last-minute planning I could pull off, I'm surprised it started out this fine.

    Nice sits in the southeast of France on the Mediterranean Sea, a key city of the French Riviera, or what we know as Côte d'Azur. It kind of reminds me a little of Portugal with its cobblestone streets and endless alleyways. I like how it is nothing like Paris, which I got to visit on our honeymoon last summer, and its old-world charm fascinated me. Tomorrow I will make my way to Monte Carlo, another city I've longed to see, but for now it's me and the sea.

    If you could live vicariously through me for just a minute, take a breath and imagine a still, vast body of water, serene and calm, unlike the choppy ocean most of us are used to.

    "What's the difference between a sea and an ocean?" I ask. "Is this a trick question?" My husband turns to me in shock. He was expecting me to know this since I've self-proclaimed to be the brains in the marriage. "The sea does not have waves like the ocean. It's calm." I roll my eyes, expecting a more philosophical answer, but for now this one will do.

    The sun rises just over the horizon where it kisses the tiny golden ripples of the sea. It is peaceful where I sit, with the occasional flock of birds speckling the cloudless sky and almost without a care in the world, nothing that could possibly shatter this version of bliss. I'm perched at the very top floor, six stories high, admiring the greatness and sucking up every ounce of God's marvelous work I possibly can, and am going to for the next five days.

Breaking the Silence

It does sound like a fairy tale, doesn't it? I've been told I am lucky. Some envy the shoes I strut in; others admire the vigor I parade. I've been told I have a great life, and it seems like I have everything anyone could possibly want. "You don't have to worry about money. Lucky you!" "You are blessed with great skin and you don't even have to work out!" "How could you understand what it's like to be hungry?"

I say they could just be right, except that they forget a very important detail of my life. If you truly did walk in my shoes, you would realize it has never been easy or lucky or carefree at all.

On May 15, 2024, I was diagnosed with invasive ductal carcinoma (a smartass way of referring to breast cancer). The call did not come as a surprise; a part of me was prepared for something to go wrong, and the fact that it was the most common type of breast cancer did not help cushion the news. When life constantly throws curveballs at you, you somehow expect the other shoe to drop.

Is this how a self-fulling prophecy works? Did I subconsciously manifest my own downfall?

I stood at the bay window of our new home that overlooks our pool in Rancho Palos Verdes, California, as little bits of my life crumbled apart. Rancho Palos Verdes has its charm as a small coastal city that sits up in the clouds of the Palos Verdes Peninsula in South Los Angeles.

Lovely and magical, truly. However, the weather is a perpetual gloom just like the ambiance surrounding me at this moment. The marine layer had just started to roll in from the Pacific Ocean, a mysterious sense of longing and pain entangled among the fog. The sky slowly turned to overcast as the sun began to take its descent behind the clouds, almost as if it no longer adored my presence. The water did not seem to hear my voice or notice my tears. The wind did not cease to grieve me nor offer me any solace. The world kept moving on, as it always does, while mine came to a standstill.

Earlier this year, on January 18, 2024, I suffered a miscarriage. I had just arrived in Coeur d'Alene, Idaho, elated by the flurries that came to greet me at the airport. The white snow made everything look so enchanted against the dark sky and it reminded me of the movie *The Chronicles of Narnia*.

They did not have one bit of snow the entire season and just as we arrived, a little snow started falling gently from the heavens. I remarried the year before after being a single mother for almost a decade. My husband and I had come to tell good news to his family that we'd been trying hard to keep secret for close to three months. However, right before we flew out of Los Angeles, my gynecologist confirmed that there was no heartbeat for the little embryo that had formed inside me. I began bleeding two days before the flight and by the evening we arrived, the pain resembled what I knew as contractions, the same squeezing anguish I felt in 2009 when I delivered my first child. Yet still, all I could marvel at as we drove into town was the gentle snowflakes that graced my skin and how the cold made everything more bearable.

By morning my world collapsed. I had broken a cold sweat in the hotel and in two hours, bled myself to a miscarriage. I spent the morning mourning the loss of our child. By noon, I had already showered and was dressed to continue the events of the day just as planned to not let anyone down or even raise an eyebrow. Once again, I picked myself up and cleansed the smear of failure and inadequacy from my aura. No one ever found out or suspected a thing for the next four days.

How lucky is that?

When I was a little girl, maybe two or three, I spent my days in a room with deep maroon carpets lined wall-to-wall, the kind that belonged in the eighties, along with bell-bottomed jeans, big hair, and fancy, neon prints. It was a large room that had toys lined across the baseboards from one corner to the other, and paintings that hung from its walls. A little wooden play structure occupied a corner and dolls of all shapes and colors and sizes were strewn across the floor. There were gifts for every occasion, and gifts for absolutely no reason at all. The epitome of a blessed childhood seemed evident and many would say I had nothing to complain about at all.

I had a pretty good childhood. I recall many good moments, lots of happy occasions, and a lot of really good food. I am blessed

Breaking the Silence

to come from an extended family of great cooks and lucky to be born in Singapore, a multicultural society that embraces food as part of their cultural identities. Two and a half years of eating and playing on my own, my sister came along and I had a best friend to experience life with. This was when we moved into a larger condominium with a swimming pool and playgrounds in a gated community. We had turtles, hamsters, frogs, fish, rabbits, chickens, and anything two little girls could imagine growing up with. We never had to try hard for much at all. Our lives seemed to be ideal, if not magical, growing up.

It was just another day at home ... tension rising high with every second that passed as the sun began to set. Our days had become burdened with the incessant shouting and cursing shortly after we moved in. The unpleasant intervals of silence were rudely interrupted by the front door creaking open. Everything happened so fast. I had barely finished dinner. It was almost bedtime; we ate late that evening. The mood was a morbid funk of enmity and ire. Everything was quiet and then it wasn't. The dense air turned into an outburst of rage and petulance. The screaming and shouting got worse with each passing second, and things were flung across the room. I grabbed my sisters and shoveled them into the hallway bath in a pathetic attempt to spare them from the nightmare that was about to unfold.

At some point, I lunged towards the bloody heap of chaos in our dining room, trying to intervene as best as I could. I was too small, too fragile. So I picked up the phone and dialed the police and my grandmother. I thought this would be the end of years of fighting, but I soon discovered that I was wrong.

My life turned into a living nightmare soon after. I do not recall a day of peace after we moved. I do not remember hearing the words that every young child longs to hear; "I love you" did not exist in our space. It became my fault for not taking sides that horrendous night and I was made to remember it as much as possible so I could never be happy or forget that incident ever.

Did I do something wrong?

I spent the next two years living in a dreadful cycle of guilt and confusion. I woke up to leave for school, wishing I never had to come back, and went to bed praying that I would not wake up. That was the time I developed chronic gastritis, and I've had it ever since. My mealtimes were never consistent; half the time I barely ate. There were no playdates, no family outings, no evening talks about my day, and definitely no hugs or kisses. At some point, there was no power, no water, no food, and nothing left to comfort me about the plight I put us in. Or did I?

The deprivation of love and affection took a toll on my self-esteem at such a tender age. The funny thing about verbal abuse is that you actually start to believe what you are told, and it becomes a part of your reality, something that you convince yourself of for as long as you can remember. I was the "parasite" who leeched off everyone, who couldn't provide or do nothing. Remember, I was merely thirteen at this time. The constant gaslighting and name-calling took an emotional toll on my mental health.

I had just started secondary school in Singapore (referred to as high school in America), but I was not enjoying my teenage years. I found comfort in the friends I met; smoking with them became a relief by the time I turned fourteen. I rarely came home on time and spent most of my evenings gallivanting in the neighborhoods.

The little incisions on my arms masked the emotional turmoil with ounces of physical pain, distracting my brain from dwelling in any psychological torture. There was a minute part of me that wanted to run the blade through my flesh, deep enough to ease the pain and end it all. Mentally, I was not strong enough to end my life and so I could only go as far as my mind would let me, far enough so I could no longer hear the enraged voice telling me how worthless I am. My only solace came from the soundless nights when I hid myself among my thoughts, sketching and writing to express my shame in the hope that someone, somewhere could save me.

It was then that I ran away. I gathered a few of my favorite things and left, and I never returned or looked back.

Forgiveness is a tricky thing, much like healing is. Alan Paton said, "When a deep injury is done to us, we never recover until we forgive." I spent my nights researching and studying the art of forgiveness and healing. For years I worked on my healing and forgave anyone who wronged me, or vice versa. For years I worked on myself, ensuring that I would not carry this with me as I aged. For years I swore that the generational trauma would end with me, here and now.

Mahatma Gandhi said, "The weak can never forgive. Forgiveness is the attribute of the strong."

I was strong.

I was twenty-two years old when I moved to the United States. I grew to become a confident, compassionate young adult with a naïve propensity to see the good in everyone. I worked hard at a promising career and had just received a promotion overseas that landed me in America. I was proud of how far I'd come. I have always been grateful for the opportunities (and blessings) that God has bestowed upon me throughout my journey. It seemed that all my efforts had paid off and life was leading me in a great direction. It wasn't long before I met a charming lad with eyes the color of the ocean and a touch so gentle that it convinced me to settle. It was the fairy tale relationship every girl wanted to have, the envy of all our peers. We soon moved into a beautiful home, the kind in a dream with a picket fence across the front lawn and fruit trees in the backyard. Little, white fluffy dogs played in the hallway that was adorned with abstract paintings, ones that you spend hours staring at, yet never really figuring out why.

Slowly, bit by bit, my life started to unravel. The good and the bad, the joy and the tears. It was a pretty dream until one faithful evening, life became all too familiar, just like it did years ago during dinner, shadowing moments of indescribable silence filled with thoughts of fear and anguish that I felt that night.

I had just set the table and was putting the finishing touches on a new dish I had been longing to try from Singapore, excited about having perfected it the first-time round. The door slammed shut just as I had set the food out and a loud bellowing followed from the front of the house. Before long, an intense argument erupted, and I was backing up into a corner of the room. It all sounded too familiar—the consistent shouting, the terrifying silences that gave hints to what would happen next. I could feel the hair stand on the back of my neck as I watched what I anticipated to be a lovely evening get torn apart with shreds of nostalgia and regret. Just like that, I was forced to relive my childhood all over again. This time, however, I was the main lead in the show.

What did I do wrong?

For the next five years, my life completely activated the parts of me that felt small, insignificant, and unlovable, the same parts of me that stemmed from my childhood years, telling me how worthless I had become. My existence had become a forlorn cause, and I was completely jaded. It was as if the incubus had woken up after decades of slumber and now sought vengeance for my leaving home at fourteen. In truth, every part of me that I had healed as a child was slowly crumbling apart again. It was my childhood on repeat, a life full of gaslighting and control. I lost all my friends and there was no family around. My career was labeled useless, and I was a good-for-nothing, just a parasite that leeched off everyone and anyone. My faith was damning, and I could barely escape to church.

The bitter evenings were compensated for by tears filled with apologies and lovely flowers. The lonely weekends came with pretty purses and shining jewelry. The roller-coaster love story became more unbearable as the nights turned to mornings, and the light turned to darkness. As much as you try to hold onto the good moments, the bad ones soon overshadow them, and you slowly lose track of whether it was ever good to begin with. It became a life of lies, one excuse after another to bury the last one and make everything seem normal again.

Within the span of two decades, I was made to relive my childhood trauma countless times that the voices in my head had started to intermingle. Now not only was there the voice that defined my worth, but there was also a second voice backing the first one up! What I thought was a blissful life turned into a contrived mental dungeon where I had to spend years fixing things I never broke, and healing wounds I did not ask for. This next sequence of events in my early adulthood activated a part of me I thought I had healed.

Breaking the Silence

I finally mustered all the courage I could find, snuck out one morning, and went back to church. For the next few hours, I wept silently in a pew, hoping no one would find me.

Society has a funny way of looking at abuse. Since I did not have broken bones and did not bleed to death, my experiences had been downplayed and I was constantly told to "get over it." The epitome of my demise was when someone insinuated that I must have done something wrong to deserve this.

It was on that note that one bright, sunny, California morning, I packed my bags and left. I ran away and never looked back ... again.

In all honesty, there is no way to tell my story in one chapter. Four thousand words is just barely enough for me to express the pain I have struggled with. I have kept myself silent, away from the public eye to protect the ones I love and to ensure that they are shielded from any repercussions of my truth. There is a stigma of shame and guilt that we sometimes carry that makes it difficult to speak our truth or use our voices.

When I learned of my diagnosis, I realized how lonely it was to be the one with cancer. Equally so, I realized how lonely I have been from carrying years of trauma inside me. I began to comprehend how so many women (and men) sit with themselves, ashamed and guilted because they are afraid of being judged. More importantly, I learned to see how anyone in either situation, whether it is disease or abuse, can continue to return to a place of misery and darkness because there is just nowhere else for them to be. Like my cancer, my trauma had led me down the same path, isolated and empty, as if the entire universe had come crashing down on me. My voice has been stifled, buried, in the depths of my breasts where my cancer breathes.

On July 12, I opted for a double mastectomy to remove the cancer cells. Physically, I endured thirteen hours of surgery that would take me months to recover from. Psychologically, I submitted to a lifelong path of healing and forgiveness, releasing past trauma, one memory at a time, that kept me bound to survival methods I no longer require and old trauma that has ridden me with disease and illness from my cancer. My body is slowly recuperating from post-cancer treatment, yet my mind and soul have been detoxing from the voices inside that have haunted me for years, the same voices that made me feel small and weak.

    Remember how I tried to find ways to heal and forgive, and even thrived after that? Well, what we don't realize about healing or forgiving is that it is a never-ending battle that requires mindfulness and self-awareness to ensure that each time we are triggered, we work on containing it, so it doesn't escalate into something out of our control. Healing is a lifelong journey, so is forgiveness. And I owe it to myself to make sure that my past and experiences do not become generational trauma that will bleed on those around me who did not cut me.

ABOUT THE AUTHOR

    Rebecca Binny is an award-winning public relations strategist who has dedicated her expertise to aiding women and minority groups to propel themselves and flourish in the corporate and nonprofit arenas. Rebecca is the recipient of Business Elite's "40 Under 40" award and Industry Innovator award for PR NEWS, as well as several other awards that have boosted her reputation as a pioneer in the Web3, public relations, and marketing space. She is passionate about bringing work opportunities to marginalized communities and elevating women in business. Her work encompasses strategies that promote diversity and embrace the need for change in the workplace. Rebecca is an entrepreneur, speaker, moderator, and writer and has been featured in *PRWeek, MoneyMade, Yahoo! Finance*, and numerous other publications. She regularly speaks at universities and private businesses on diversity, Web3, and communications.

    Rebecca has a master's in Communication Management from the University of Southern California and serves as advisor for Women in Leadership at the University of California-Riverside, Extension. She previously served as advisor for Design Thinking at the University of California-Riverside, Extension. Originally from Singapore, she is currently based in South Bay,

Breaking the Silence

Los Angeles where she advocates for equality and diversity, and uses her voice to fight against domestic violence.

Rebecca's story is depicted in her first book release in spring of 2025. You can follow along her endeavors and stories online via Instagram and Facebook by searching for "Rebecca Binny" or using the links below.

Instagram: https://www.instagram.com/rebecca.binny/
Facebook: https://www.facebook.com/rebeccabinny/

CHAPTER 17

THE MANY STORIES OF SURVIVAL

Jennifer Dall

Kintsugi is the Japanese art of mending broken ceramics with gold. I feel like I am a broken ceramic plate, just getting to the part of rebuilding with gold.

One Saturday in April 2022, I came home from a yoga class and my whole life changed. I walked into a tragic situation that I never would have believed possible. After almost twenty-nine years of marriage, my husband had decided to take his own life. As I found out, this is unfortunately far from uncommon, but also something that no one wants to talk about. As I write this it has been more than two years since he died, but the story of survival continues every day.

This is my story and I'm telling it to encourage *you* to tell your story in its rawest form. Even more than that, to share that I think that our stories, which must be understood and told, can sometimes come out better when we take a step away from the drama, the facts, add a touch of heart and creativity, and find a way to also tell the story that shows emotions, respect, grace, and creativity to any and all of those involved. I need to tell my story like this, to tell my story the way I want. This story comes first; we create beauty with it later.

These are the facts. The truth. This is one way to see the truth.

The Past

My husband and I married in August in the early 1990s and began our lives together. We had a child, a wonderful daughter, and first one dog, then another. We lived in the same small house on a quiet street in the foothills for the entire time. We did the usual things: work on the house and yard, spend time with friends and family, travel a little, go to work, live our lives. We had very little drama or tragedy in our lives.

Breaking the Silence

Sometimes it's hard to remember much of that time. One thing I learned about trauma and grief is that they play games with your mind and your memories. After almost twenty-nine years I feel like one day, one simple brief day, erased so much of that time in my mind.

Still there are memories, crystal clear things that I remember: a trip to Catalina Island shortly after we met; all the hours and years on small house projects like painting, gardening, planting flowers and produce; two dogs that we raised—a dalmatian and a black-and-tan coonhound/shepherd mix; a wonderful daughter that we brought into this world; camping trips, softball games, and traveling to marathons. Day after day, the consistency of being in our house, our family, our relationship built a lifetime together that I thought would never end. In almost thirty years, these are some of the things I remember. I don't always remember all the details very well. It's always been like that.

That day I remember in several ways. There are visions in sharp focus and in a blur, and finally I see things as if I'm looking down from above on these actors in a strange play. The pandemic years were not good for any of us. Things happened that impacted our future lives. On that day in April 2022, it started off pretty normal. It was a sunny Saturday morning, and I went to a yoga class nearby. I was proud because work and life stress made going out challenging and I did a lot of this. I went and I felt proud. I showed up for the class and stayed and looked forward to coming again regularly. I thought things were starting to get back to pre-pandemic normal.

The last memories I have of my husband are of him cleaning the window on the car as I tried to rush off so I wouldn't be late to the class. I also remember us planning for my daughter, my husband, and I to do something that afternoon together. I remember that the night before, we took our dog for a walk. It struck me even then as odd because it was a different walk, reversed of our regular path. He made a nice pasta dinner and had a couple of glasses of wine. This was different, also. He rarely drank much. Maybe I'm looking back and reading into the night, trying to make meaning of it.

Breaking the Silence

    I remember that morning, asking him what he was going to do, and his response was an uncharacteristic, "Stay home alone, I guess." That morning as I got out of bed to do my morning writing, he asked me to come back and stay and I said, "I need to go write." I often wonder if only I had done this one thing, maybe things would have been different, even though I know that it was not just one thing. Other memories are hazy as to when they happened in the day or days before his death.
    One time he was angry and suspicious about a friend I was talking to. We were catching up since she'd retired and was asking for information about early retirement. A stupid fight about one of the cars. Fights about me working or retiring and starting my coaching business full-time. We were still recovering from a pandemic, his stroke, his mother's death, and his decision to retire early.
    Here's what was different about my husband. He had a stroke in August of 2020. He spent a few nights in the hospital and was released. Every medical person claimed the tests showed he was fine, that there were no complications from the stroke. From then on, he was different though. He became more forgetful, paranoid, and angry. He refused to get help, refused to go to a doctor. The times he tired, he denied that anything was wrong and the doctors accepted it. My daughter and I saw it. We just didn't know what we were seeing.
    On that day in April 2022, I came home from yoga. I really wanted a hug from him, but he wasn't in the house. The back door was open a little. The dog came out of her doghouse. Something seemed off. It was quiet. So quiet. I looked at the computer as I walked in where he often left notes: "Took T for a walk," "Out for a ride," "Went to park or store." Nothing. I walked around our house and called out his name. Nothing but silence. I went to the backyard where he would work on the plants. Nothing. I checked the front yard where he would stand or talk to a neighbor. I hadn't noticed anything. I walked around the inside of the house again, the dog following me in silence. I called his cell phone. No answer and no ring that I could hear, and it went straight to voicemail, as if

Breaking the Silence

he'd left it and stepped out for a minute. I felt odd. The whole place felt hollow.

The first logical conclusion was that he went for a walk or possibly a bike ride. Lacking a note or a phone there was no way to know if he'd gone for a walk, although he usually took the dog along. I wondered if he went for a bike ride, so I pressed the button to open the garage door to see if his bike was there. Weird. I remember thinking. I'd never done that before and wasn't sure why I thought to check for the bike.

I could open the door from the kitchen. I pushed the button and started walking out the back door, down the cement path next to the house, and out the chain link gate. I pushed open the gate a thousand times before and saw him in the garage. It looked like he was standing on the ladder getting something out of the eaves. I remember thinking, "Oh, he must be working on the inside of the garage door opener, something must be wrong with it." That was odd, but I was glad I found him.

Then I saw. I really SAW. Just know this is a vision that will never leave my mind. He had chosen to use a krypton bike chain to hang himself. The ladder was right there. His favorite car was right there. I still believe he could have put his feet down, but who knows if that was true?

I called 911. I tried to lift him up to lessen the pressure. I kept saying, "NO, NO, NO!" I knew it was too late. I don't really know how long it took them to arrive. I know I paced the driveway. I kept saying, "No, no, what did you do?" I called our daughter. "I need you to come home!" The only neighbor to come and try to help was the man across the street; they used to talk to each other a lot.

The police and fire department arrived and asked so many questions. We said, "We didn't know." Sure, there were things that had been challenging, but we had no idea. No idea at all. We had plans. I just went to a yoga class. I was only gone a little over an hour. The dog was upset about all the people.

My daughter's friend stayed and sat with us, running interference, getting water for the dog, watching over as we waited in a corner of the front yard where we could not see down the

Breaking the Silence

driveway and into the garage. At some point I slipped into the house, avoiding looking out any back window to see the garage, to quickly change. ... I was still in yoga clothes.

I remember the coroner's staff asking us, "Do you want to see him before we take him?" This was directed at me and at my daughter, whose last sight of him was earlier that morning when he was perfectly fine. We decided she didn't want to remember him any other way.

Later that day we drove her friend back to her dorm. I still see us sitting at a Thai restaurant we'd never been to, in shock, trying to eat a little, trying to figure out what to do next. Hoping to wake up from the nightmare. We decided to stay in the house that night and another friend brought a blow-up mattress. The first night we spent in my daughter's room together, sleeping with the dog.

I started calling some people that night, those I thought would understand and help. I arranged for a friend to come the next day, and both of us felt unable to process any of it. The next night I stayed at that friend's house. I started sobbing in the morning alone before she woke up. Then I escaped to another house, a friend on maternity leave.

And then I went home. The outside world started to intrude for a bit. A few neighbors wanted to know how we were. A DoorDash gift card dropped off. Calls came from people we hadn't heard from in years. People wanted to know all, and of course, if we needed anything, just let them know. We didn't know then how quickly all of that would stop and leave us in silence. Numbness for days, escaping to the mountains, the beach, San Francisco, other places ... all the decisions.

"What do I do now?"

For me this story is visual, a very visual, visceral story. I see images and to this day it plays out like a storyboard of a really bad movie. Visions, scenes, in between numbness and confusion, and not understanding.

Our survival path was and still is a struggle. There was so much to do and so much I didn't want to do. Do I want to stay in this house, where I can't look at the garage? The one my daughter was raised in, the one our whole married life was spent in? The one filled with his things and our things?

I went out looking for a new house in the city. There were bidding wars and extremely high prices. Plus, I'd have to put my house on the market. I thought of burning the garage down. I wondered if a minor earthquake could just destroy that. Ultimately I decided to hire a company to design and oversee the remodel of it into a study for me to work in and maybe a friend to stay in. It's almost done and all I can think is that maybe it's time to leave. Working on the house was at times cathartic. Working through the pain while working on the house.

There were arguments with the cell phone company about a phone he'd recently bought on a payment plan. They wouldn't let me into the account, yet still wanted me to pay off the phone. A friend, who happens to be a lawyer, just happened to be with us and they gave her a hard time. I was using his medical insurance, which I found out later had been cut off the first of the month, as he died on the thirtieth, but they didn't tell me until calls and bills with a therapist had built up.

Handing over his death certificate was both devastating and surreal to human resources at both of our employers, financial institutions, attorneys, and all of them seeing in bold black letters the cause of death.

I quit my job I'd been in for almost the same amount of time and took a job in a different school district because I believed a change would be good. Was it good? It was a change. It was horrible working on a high school campus with its own mental health challenges and by the holidays I had turned in papers for my own early retirement. I was unable to complete projects, plan for the future, know what to do or what I want. I was hiding my feelings from almost everyone because no one really understood.

The Present

This is also the truth. There are times that are rough and times that are not as rough. It is all still very much a struggle. As I write this, my daughter is truly moving into her adult life. She is working towards beginning a graduate degree in a beautiful college town several hours away from me. I've enjoyed being invited in to help her create her first own space in a very cute apartment that is perfect for her. I've released myself to create a new space and life for myself. The garage that I once could not look at is almost complete as an expanded work studio for me to create all the projects and life that I deserve and will work hard for. Some days I hate it all and can't stop crying.

    I am a very different person than I was before this happened. I wonder if I am closer to the person I was as a kid, but I still think it is a different person even from that. Being a different person means that so much of my past life no longer fits. This hurts a lot and is confusing. So many people I knew no longer fit in my life. Neighbors I've shared a street with for so long avoid me. His friends, our couple friends, have all disappeared. I believe they do not know what to say and choose to say nothing, to see nothing. I also believe that suicide hits way too close to home. They don't want to see it and think that it could cross their lives.

    This separation continues to adult friends that I've known for years, for most of them there is nothing to say. They have no idea. They ask how I am and what answer is there but "Okay?" If I tell the truth, they feel they must solve it, when all I want is to be seen, to have space held. If I say, "Doing well," to protect them, they believe it is always and forever okay. So, there is really no one I even bother to talk to.

    There are a few exceptions, and they are interesting and comforting. One was my maid of honor, someone I have known since middle school. For so long we fell adrift. We lived far away from each other, had kids, lived our own lives and traumas, and drifted for no other reason than lack of follow through. We connected after his death and have since texted, visited, attended concerts together. There does seem to be some acceptance in the fact that we know the younger, more innocent versions of each other, have missed such a large chunk of growth and trauma, and yet seem to be able to hold space in this new world.

    Another woman my husband and I spent a lot of time with for several years. She was divorced; the men were the original friends so we lost each other but she also came back after the death. She is another who knew a certain version of me. We've both been through incredible experiences and are now figuring out how to move forward with grief and loss. My best friend is someone I hardly knew, who I had just met through a coaching training in the months before he died. We have a background that is both frighteningly similar and very different. She has shown a compassion and openness that I can never repay. Finally, a person I met right at the beginning of the end, during the start of the pandemic, who endured her own tragedy at the same time as I did. While we know certain parts of each other, what we know best is that we are both humbled by the experiences that led us to surviving the grief that we feel.

    I am allowing myself time to learn, to create, to relearn, to be reborn. Finding new friends is hard, taking care of myself is hard, writing this chapter, my books, creating my programs, starting a new relationship—these are all hard. The big thing I've learned is to take it step by step. If I remember that I will feel different in a little while, that each step, no matter how small, is still a step forward, I keep making progress.

    I started dating someone, but this has been a very difficult road. I've told very few people, mostly because we don't have deep conversations and they don't ask about anything that is not superficial. This is hard but what's worse is that my daughter is having none of it. I wonder if I'm sabotaging the relationship and I think I wouldn't have spent time on the other side of this. I know my daughter is looking out for me and is not understanding it from my point of view.

    I wonder if staying in the house is the right thing to do. Soon the entire landscaping will be redone and it will be a beautiful restful space to work and relax and share with a few close friends.

    Every time I drive up the main street leading to my house, my heart freezes. Often I check out and have a hard time remembering to breathe. I think of finding a new place. Yes, I made this mine, but the framework and foundation are still the same, and not one that I ever selected on my own. I think of starting new elsewhere. Even somewhere else in this city that I do

Breaking the Silence

love. At times I hate all of it. I wonder what happened and why and I don't know how else to proceed.

I wonder how my daughter tells her story, for hers is inherently different from mine. She is a daughter, not a wife. She is still a daughter, and now I am a widow. Her future decisions don't involve making a totally new life from scratch or using gold to meld the pieces back together. Her future life is building on. Yes, one of her anchors is gone, but she will be fine. I know that the story I tell today is not the end. I have the future and so much of that is unknown.

This is not the story I want to tell. There must be meaning at least for those of us remaining. Looking at it so brutally, the details, the facts, the memories are ugly and harsh. What I want moving forward is to tell this in a way that someone can learn from. That someone can relate to the human experience. Yes, step one is survival. Step two is living one step away from survival. Step three may be the facts, the data, the science, but the story I need to tell, that I believe brings it home to a place that you can use, is turning to creativity. Take the raw materials and make the story something that you can live with, turn it into something ephemeral, global, transcendent.

The Future

This, this too is the truth. As I sit here today, anxiously, excitedly watching the days go by and the small steps that I'm taking add up to yards and miles, I can't believe that I'm actually here. It feels both happy and exciting and tragic. I'm sharing my story of survival and speaking to audiences about it. I'm working with motivating professionals to hone my story, learn to tell it, and bring my story to the world for both a way to share and help and to also encourage women to learn, find, and creatively tell their own stories. There are days that telling this story feels healthy and right and I know I am reaching out to people who need it. There are days when the pain returns and it's like it just happened.

To tell a story you must know your truth behind it and that is often hidden from us. To tell a story, you must see the past as it was then and as it is to you now. To tell a story you must creatively bring it forward into your present and your future. The trauma, the survival does not go away. The pain from it is still there, yet I believe I needed to hear painfully honest stories and that others do too.

ABOUT THE AUTHOR

Dr. Jennifer Dall is a Grief Informed Neurodivergence Specialist for people who are ready to stop the daily struggle—with ADHD and with grief—and find themselves. Through her social media, blogs, radio show and podcast, and guest podcast appearances, she serves an audience of thousands. Jennifer delivers advice on not simply surviving grief with an ADHD brain, but also discovering your personal ADHD and grief story to thrive in life. Dr. Dall is a former teacher with twenty-five years of experience, a certified ADHD coach and yoga teacher, trained grief educator, a parent, widow, and late-in-life ADHD woman. When Jennifer is not coaching, creating, writing, and sharing about ADHD and grief, she can be found traveling and exploring far and wide, relaxing with her friends, family, and pup in her newly redone home, reading, and dreaming up new things to try.

If you are called to learn more about your ADHD and grief please follow her on Instagram @adhd.holistically or go to www.adhdholistically.com to get access to her mailing list. There you will find information about publications, coaching, and other opportunities.

CHAPTER 18

SURVIVING THE DECISIONS AND OUTCOMES

Vivian E. Lopez

Trauma is a strong word and means different things to different people. I define trauma as something that changed my life and something that I can truly never forget. It always plays a part in the back of mind, even now. Looking back, I had plenty of trauma by the time I was thirteen, but all of that was out of my control and things, I thought, were normal. It wasn't until I was in my late teens that I realized that they weren't, but that is a story for another time.

I often ask myself, "How did I get here?" I mean here at this point of life, which I am thankful for finally after years and years. I am happy and at peace. However, it took years of work and it's still a work in progress because I wanted to do so much more and only now am I realizing I can. My life is not over, and I can do what I want. I ask myself again, "How did I get here and where do I want to go?"

My daughter often jokes that it is because I married their father—the only benefit of that marriage was the birth of my two amazing children. My son and my daughter, who are my entire world. I would not be here to even write this chapter without them. While I agree with my daughter, after all these years of questioning and doing the hard work and looking inside of myself, surrounded by the people around me, I realized it was because of the trauma I endured. My rapist, who I thought was my friend, and the man (dragon) I thought God sent to save me and be my hero and protector, was not a hero or protector at all but instead caused many, many of my struggles and trauma.

I had to take a hard look at my past and realized no matter what trauma occurred, I first had to make a choice. I would say the first choice I really made on my own was at thirteen. My decision caused me the most trauma, maybe because it was made by peer pressure and not being able to understand when someone wanted to harm me. When someone that I trusted, and thought was my friend was really out to hurt me.

The day my life really changed, I was thirteen years old. So much had happened in my home in that same year. I was still pushing forward. The day life changed was when my friend and I cut school (well, half of the school day) to go to a party. At least, we thought it was a party. Our two male friends tricked us and told us there was a big cut-party going on and even the guys that we liked were going to be there. We believed them because the guy I liked was not in school. Nor was he answering his beeper.

Stupidly (or should I say naively) we left and went with them. When we got to the apartment, it was to our surprise no one was there. We asked why and they told us that they were at another location but were on the way, and they begged us to stay. Again, young and naïve, so we stayed. One of the guys offered us something to drink like water or orange juice and we both said orange juice. I noticed it tasted different, but I just thought it was different, maybe more expensive, unlike the ninety-nine cent OJ I was used to. I never drank alcohol or did any drugs, so I didn't know it was alcohol

I remember I got so sleepy and next thing I knew I was awoken by my friend screaming in the next room and this man I thought was my friend on top of me holding me down. And then this weird new feeling that hurt—he was inside of me. I screamed, I tried to push him off, but I was so weak and tired, I couldn't do anything. Once he finished, he left the room. I heard him and his friend talking in the hallway and they left the apartment. My friend and I screamed for each other, got dressed, and ran out of the apartment and out of the building. We went to the staircase and just cried for a while, then to a public bathroom and cleaned up. We swore we wouldn't tell our parents because they would just say it was our fault for cutting school. The sad thing is neither one of us had adults we could confide in or help us.

My innocence was taken. I never even had tongue-kissed a boy before I had my virginity stolen. I had no idea what to do. I felt so alone and so distorted. I remember I kept saying to myself, "How I did let this happen, how could I be so dumb?" To make matters worse, the guy I really liked didn't believe me when I told him a few days later what happened. He accused me of willingly sleeping with the monster because he wasn't around. Instead of being mad at my attacker or going to protect me, he said, "Well at least you're not a virgin anymore so you should have no problem having sex with me." I was shocked and heartbroken. Now, I was traumatized twice by one event and had no one to really help me deal with or process it.

    I can say I was traumatized three times by this one event. Nineteen years later, I was forced to join social media and the monster actually requested to be my friend, as if nothing ever happened. Everything came rushing back to me and I was not okay. At this point in my life, I had the knowledge that I didn't need to self-medicate with alcohol, but instead called someone and talked about it. I thought I had put the past behind me, but the truth is you cannot run from your past. That only makes it worse. You must work and deal with it to become stronger, to be better.

    As they say, every action has a reaction, and for the rest of my teen years my reaction was me turning cold and bitter. I would even say reckless at times as I would stop caring about the important things. I stopped caring about my own life. I did things I never thought I would, like not going to school or going to school just to fight in the wars we would have with the other neighborhoods or partying with alcohol. My entire personality changed after that day. I was barely eating or sleeping, and there were no adults to help support or guide me or even notice there was something wrong.

    Within a few months, I was sent away to go live with family. It was either that or go to a group home. I had gotten so out of control in some of my actions that I only had those two choices. Let's just say going to live with family made matters worse, and the situation could have had me in real trouble, so within a year I was back home. However, I was different. I had to sleep on a sofa bed and I realized I had to really fend for myself. There was no adult in my life at the time who cared enough about me to really see what was going on. So, I went back to school. I did summer and night school to catch up so I could graduate on time. I got two

Breaking the Silence

jobs, so I was able to save money and buy things I wanted and needed. I graduated at the age of seventeen and in the summer after graduation, a friend and I were able to move out into our own apartment. I was able to start college without any help from my family, filling out applications or even FAFSA applications and kept my two jobs to be able to pay rent. I was also fortunate enough to have some inheritance that helped me buy a car and keep my bills paid. I was a true adult, and I would say for a seventeen-year-old, I was killing it. I was grown, I was happy, and I was making my own decisions.

At the age of eighteen, I had my breaking point. All the years of trauma from childhood, disappointment, and heartbreak finally got to me. I was burnt out. I was going around for years as if I was strong and didn't have a care in the world. Then it happened: just when I thought my heart couldn't break any more, it did. I remember the day like it was yesterday, and there are days my heart still breaks because of it.

I remember coming home from work. I was truly exhausted because of my daily routine, at least so I thought. I didn't even think it could have been anything else. I went to the bathroom, and I was so sick. My roommate asked if we should go to the hospital because I could barely stand. At first I said no, and then I agreed we would go to the ER, and after a few hours I was seen.

The doctor came back to tell me I was pregnant. How could I have been pregnant when I was on the pill? Not only was I pregnant but I was so far along that I only had two weeks to choose whether or not to keep the baby. This didn't make any sense. The father was gone, and I was unable to get in touch with him. We were in love at one point but circumstances at the time caused us to no longer be together. I had to make a choice fast. I sat for days, just crying and trying to figure out what to do. I was so young, I was working so much, partying when I could, and barely could take care of myself let alone a child. I decided to have the abortion because I thought it would be the best thing for me. I can't speak for other women, but I will say that was the hardest thing I ever had to do in my life, even to this day.

Breaking the Silence

After the abortion, I truly lost it. I couldn't forgive myself and for days didn't want to get out of bed. I was in so much emotional pain that I decided that day I didn't want to live anymore. I didn't deserve to live anymore. So, I broke. I took two bottles full of over-the-counter aspirin followed by a bottle of rum and I laid on the floor crying until I passed out. As I laid there, all I could recall thinking about was my baby that I just aborted. Much to my surprise I was woken up by my stomach being pumped with charcoal. I was screaming at the doctors to let me die. I wanted to see my baby and I wanted to see my grandmother who passed away when I was thirteen right before the rape.

They brought me back to the world. It turns out, two of my friends came over to check on me when they said they called me and I didn't sound good earlier in the day. I don't even recall talking to them. However, they saved my life in more ways than one. I was kept on a seventy-two-hour hold, but it was the best thing because that was when I found out there was help out there. There was someone to talk to and my journey to self-healing started … at least so I thought.

A few months, almost a year goes by, and I was now nineteen, about to be twenty. I was going to therapy bi-weekly to get the help I needed. Boom, another curveball. I thought I met someone who truly cared for me, and I mean just cared for me as a person. Instead, it was yet another monster. When we met, I knew it wasn't love, it was just two broken people who somehow became very dependent on each other and shared each other's pain and suffering. I was blinded and moved too quickly. One night meeting the monster turned into six years full of hell and ten years of having to rebuild. I had no clue who the monster truly was, but he was toxic. He tricked me into believing that he wanted a wife and a family, but that was not true and I had no clue what I was getting into.

I believe because we both came from broken, toxic homes we could be smarter and could make a family work. We did it for a while, until the pressure got to him and he was no longer able to balance both a family and the street life he wanted to live. His decision cost me and my children so much more. In the middle of giving birth to my two children, we lost a child because of all the stress and hell I was going through. Of course, I felt it was my fault and I was getting fed up.

I am not going to get into details in this chapter. But I will say another reason I had issues sleeping at night was because of the time I was sound asleep only to wake up to knocking on the door and five to ten police officers tearing our house apart. They went through and trashed every part of our apartment including our kids' clothes and woke my children out of their beds. I think the most memorable thing was when they went into our fridge and checked every inch, including where the eggs go. This is most likely one of the reasons why I am so OCD clean now. While I cannot speak for him, I will say he made the decision to choose the streets over his family and ended up being sentenced for a long time in prison. This has cost us a lot. Not just our reputation, but financially it left us stuck, left my children with no father and me with no help to raise my children. His mother and brother didn't do a thing to help us or even see or call to check up on my children.

I had to make some hard and tough decisions, I had two kids to raise; they were only two and four at the time. We were one step from being homeless and tossed into a shelter. I had no clue he was behind a month on our rent and had tickets and issues with all three of the cars. To the outside person, they thought we were living great. Even I thought we were good. I was working, he was working, so how could we be so far behind?

I truthfully will never forgive him or his mother for what they did to my children. However, I had to move on, and I couldn't let my children suffer for my mistake of marrying their father. In some ways I ended up very happy being a single mother and not having to co-parent or deal with the other person's drama. I am not advocating to have more single mothers; if you can make being together or co-parenting work, I highly recommend it. However, for me single motherhood worked.

It was not easy by any means, and I ended up having a village to help me. However, I was able to break barriers and provide a life for them that most people could not. My children have experienced things that I only had dreamed of as a kid. Just as

Breaking the Silence

simple as them having their own rooms most of their lives. When their father got locked up, we had to move in with my mother, of all people, into a one-bedroom apartment. The home I fled at seventeen, I returned to and now with two children. I needed the help but so did she, as she was going through her own financial situation and breakup.

I am grateful my mother was there for my kids, and she is and has always been a way better grandmother than she was a mother. I am blessed for that. My kids and I slept in the living room. It was sometimes even hard for me to imagine how we had three beds and two dressers in the living room, but we did it. We struggled for years. I was in school finishing my master's and then had enough of New York and decided I wanted to get my kids out of there. I love the Bronx, but I wanted more for my kids. I wanted them to live life and not just survive.

Once I finished my master's, I decided to take my former boss up on her offer to get out of New York and move to Florida. Within two weeks I made the decision to leave the city and left all my friends and family. I was also engaged to an amazing man, but he didn't want to leave New York. Although he I felt he was the first man that made me feel truly loved unconditionally, I had to sacrifice and do what I had to. It was what I thought was best for my children. And it was the best decision.

I would not say I haven't questioned some of my choices, but I will not live in regret. I often think about how different my life would have been if I had a support system, parents, family, or any adult that would have been there for me and helped me prior or even after the rape. I try my best to be that adult, not only for my children, but for all children. I taught my children that they can come to me no matter what, and I have always been so present that others would say I was a Supermom or helicopter mom. The bond that I have with my children is so much different than I have ever had or even seen some of my friends have today. I will not sit and say my children didn't have trauma, because no matter how hard I tried at the end of the day I can't take away my past and who their father is. The past did not define me or them. We have excelled and have accomplished things that most people have not.

Especially people like us. I could not be prouder of what young adults my children have become.

    I will implore all parents to be there for your children and make sure they know you are there for them. You don't have to be perfect, but you have to be present and in the know. You cannot always protect your children from the monsters, but you can be there to help them through and teach them that there are true monsters that are not in the form of scary ghosts and goblins. but in the form of human beings.

    Remind yourself every day that the biggest revenge to all that have harmed you is success. Live your success and not regret. Your past or your family's past does not define your future. You define your future. Only you can choose whether to get up, do the work, and be happy. You have to live life in the best way you feel fit in your being, not what others have put on you. Live within your truth and things that truly make you happy.

ABOUT THE AUTHOR

    Vivian E. Lopez is a devoted single mother of two amazing children. Vivian was able to balance a full-time career and unexpected motherhood where some may have folded after dealing with so much. In addition to her amazing career, Vivian has a bachelor's in business and a master's in education. Vivian has survived a difficult childhood and early adulthood. However, she has been able to survive and thrive in this world. Although Vivian still has work to do, she is a true success story.

CHAPTER 19

DOMESTIC VIOLENCE FROM THE CHILD'S PERSPECTIVE

Tierra Carter

On January 31, 1995, my mother lost her life after a long relationship and battle with domestic violence, after dating my father from her teenage years until the day she decided enough was enough and moved us into our grandfather's house. My mother had moved us away while my father was working—he was a truck driver. My father came home to a home without his family. This was enough to make any man crazy, but my father was not just any man; he was a man with a domestic violence demon who lived within him.

My father was a very prideful man. He was a ladies' man, as people would say at that time. As a truck driver, my father made lots of money. Everyone in the neighborhood looked up to him for being a great provider and the way he loved my mother. No one really had an idea of all the things that what went on at home. Until there was nothing anyone could really do about it besides pick up the pieces that were left, which were me and my baby brother at the time.

I understood that my dad murdered my mom. I had seen and heard so many things go on between my mother and my father that I thought this was just another thing and we would be okay again. Unfortunately, not this time. Mommy would never return.

I remember the song "Waterfalls" by TLC and the song by Fugees "Killing Me Softly" playing on the radio as my grandmother drove us to the hospital to check and make sure my mother would recover from her gunshot wounds. She drove to Tampa General Hospital where they attempted to save my mother. I remember the long hallway where me, my grandmother, and my family stood and waited for the doctors to tell us the update of her surgery.

My father shot my mother, from what I remembered. I heard the gun go off five times, but according to her death certificate there were two shots that were fatal. One to her lungs and one in her back. My father owned a 22-gauge handgun at that time. As the doctors were patching and trying to stop the bleeding the bullets travelled, causing more and more damage.

While in that long hallway I heard a soft, still voice speak to me and say, "Mommy is gone." I know now at the age of thirty-three that voice was the Holy Spirit telling me what was to come. I even shared with my family, and as everyone said, "Don't say that," the doctor came out with tears in his eyes. He was completely exhausted as they had worked on my mother for at least an hour. From what I remember, he didn't even want to utter the words to my grandmother. We all cried and then I couldn't even hear anyone's cries or screams. As a child, for some reason, I believed somehow, she would come back to us or reappear that night.

We went home with our maternal grandmother, which was not out of the norm for us because my mother had sickle cell disease and so she often visited the ER and got admitted to the hospital. So, my grandmother or aunt would come get us until she got better. In my mind, this was just one of those visits; she would return. Nope, not this time. Me and my baby brother cried and cried and cried many days after for about six months of living with our grandmother. It really dawned on us—she is never coming back. Even though I saw her lifeless body, kissed her cold lips, and even sat in the casket with her, I still had hope that my mother would come home.

The night my father decided to end my mother's life, he was in a jealous rage. My father stuck with his story for many years. His story was that he was only showing my mother how to use the gun for protection, but the real story was backed up with evidence. The bullet to her back shows that the victim attempted to get away or run away. To show someone a weapon, that person would have it in their hand, not pointed at their back.

The effects of this trauma caused me nightmares, bed wetting, anger that would often be expressed at school due to other children teasing me. They would talk about how skinny I was and then revert to "Your Momma" jokes, which resulted in me going into a rage, biting, scratching and fighting.

Breaking the Silence

It was in second grade that I learned to journal in a diary about my feelings and emotions, the feelings of the loss of my mother and my father. Everything was not always bad with my father. I remember my father trying to teach us the "Lord's Prayer" on the days that he would be home and not on the road driving. I remember fishing trips where he would catch coolers and buckets of fish with a cast net over small bridges. I remember him picking us up from daycare in his huge giant semi-truck with the loudest horn in America, which my brother and I wanted to blow as if it was a toy. Every time my dad did that, we felt like we were on top of the world, like when he picked us up in his arms.

My father is 6'4". If you ever get to see me in person you will see I stole my father's features but not his height. I still feel like he's at the top of the world and I'm down at the bottom at 5'5". If you're wondering how this happened to me, especially with my mother being 5'9", my answer is all of my grandmothers are short. I know with the fireball attitude and boldness, if I were that tall the world would have kicked me out. I would be too much for society to handle. All glory be to God.

My father was angry and possessed by demonic forces. He had no clue, but my mother did. I remember one time my dad went into such a rage my mother called the police on him because he was trying to beat her while my mother's youngest sister was there. I told my mother I hated my father. I hated his guts, I said, and my mother scolded me and told me, "Don't you ever, ever, ever let me hear you say that ever again. That is your daddy and you are to always love him no matter what."

My mother never taught us to hate or feel resentment towards my father for his actions, although my father did some very hatful things to her. Like taking her medication that she needed to manage her sickle cell disease, turning the heater on to cause her to have seizures due to her disease, hit her, and even attempting to kill her twice before he did. The one time that I can recall we were living in a duplex apartment which was a one-story building with only two dwellings. They were arguing about a woman my father was seeing behind her back and I heard his gun go off. She didn't get hit and I don't know how she was able to calm him down or if he just maybe hit her with the gun and the gun went off. All I remember is the words, "I will kill you," and hearing my mother's screams.

I loved my father, but I hated his demons, and because of that I never talked to my father. He thought I was mute at one point because anytime he came around, I would shut down and not say anything. I was very angry and afraid of my father even prior to losing my mother. My anger caused me to lash out at him or shut down on him and say brave things. Deep down I was always terrified.

I remember my mother packing while my father was away, and us moving into my grandfather's house. She had dressed up our room as the characters Barney and Baby Bop. My brother liked Barney and I liked Baby Bop. My mother's room was black and red with white polka dots and filled with white and red teddy bears.

My mother was an amazing, loving mother. She loved family, she loved all her friends, and she always tried to love and help everyone. She always tried to show them the bigger picture or a brighter side to their problems despite what their situation may be. My mother hid her battle with domestic violence from many people. When some heard of her passing, they had no clue my mother endured the things she endured within the relationship. I remember the day of my mother's funeral. There were so many people who came from as far as South Carolina to support my grandmother, it was remarkable. The love that was poured out was incredible. She had some of her doctors and even people that worked in the local deli attend and pay their respects. The church was packed as if a celebrity had passed away. There were some people sitting and lots of people standing and even waiting outside to come in and view her and pay their respects.

I remember being passed around like a baby doll and given lots of kisses and hugs from those who attended. I remember my hair being in the very last hair style my mother would ever do, my hair in the small white beads in my face. I hated when my mother combed and styled my hair. My mother had no fingernails, so her grip while braiding was very tight, but I always lit up like a

Breaking the Silence

butterfly every time she finished. She always had different color beads and I use to love the sound they made when I ran through the house. My mother was a great mother. An unforgettable and incredibly thoughtful daughter, a very loving and caring sister, and to have her as a friend was a complete honor. From what I hear, she was somewhat of the glue to our family.

My mother wasn't a fighter or even a person to be known for confrontations. She wanted everyone to love one another no matter what and she was going to love you even if she only had one breath left to do it. That's the type of mother I had, a true living angel. I don't say this because she was my mother, I say this because of the loving legacy she left behind that I try so hard to live up to. Now I know my mother possessed the love of God, the love of finding no fault, no wrong, just loving and meeting people right where they were.

Because of her disease, my mother had days where she laid in bed because the pain was so unbearable. On the days she was graced to have strength, she spent showing and spreading love. Often through family night at her home where she liked to have crab shala, lasagna, and spaghetti as she loved to bring family together and have a good time; she loved to dance and make people laugh.

As a child growing up, I often felt like a burden and a misfit because others had both parents in their lives, or at least their mother. I had to always explain why my grandmother was showing up and not my parents. At first it was kind of embarrassing having my granny show up to parent teacher conferences but then I became okay with it because my teachers would always make me feel extra special once my grandmother explained the circumstances. My grandmother was like my first real teacher after daycare because she had to battle my father's family in a custody case to keep us, which I later learned was my mother's wishes prior to her death. She visited my grandmother crying and begging for her to take care of us if anything was to ever happen to her. I can only imagine what thoughts ran through my mother's head, not knowing if she was going to lose her battle of trying to live life to sickle cell disease or the nasty disease of domestic violence.

My grandmother taught me my ABC's and my numbers as well as multiplication, division, and how to read. I can remember her popping me every time I got a word wrong or attempted to say it without sounding it out. I thank God for her because of her teachings at home. Although I was behind in school, after a week in first grade the school decided I was too smart and they tested me out of first grade to second.

I remember my Aunty Gina taking me to class with all these kids that were the same age group as myself. She gave me a kiss and said, "Don't be scared." I struggled the first month, but as my grandmother began to teach me the new level, I began to like school and enjoyed learning. Even now, learning is very therapeutic to me and gives me a sense of excitement. I know I get this from both my mother and my father. I was often told how smart and organized and witty my mother was. It was just her health that stopped her from being and accomplishing many things.

Later on, I went on to middle school, which often felt weird because now I was with the nosey group of kids that wanted to know why I was always talking about my grandmother. "Is your momma a crack head?" Most times they apologized after they found out that my mother had passed away. Many didn't want to hear the story, but some would get me by myself and ask, "What happened to your momma?"

It was in my adolescent years that I became depressed. My depression got worse after experiencing a rape by a family friend at the age of thirteen and then meeting a guy by the name of Jay who acted as though he was interested in me styling his toddler's hair, only to molest me. All of this occurred because I lacked love, attention, finances, and real guidance in my home, in my education, and even in my church.

Although my maternal great-grandmother often took me to church and added me to the children's church choir, no one really discussed life with me or my feelings. Everyone always gave me the cold shoulder. "You're a child and you don't have real problems because you don't pay any bills and your only job is to

Breaking the Silence

go to school and get good grades, graduate, and go to college and become something great." Jay listened to me, he kissed me, he hugged me, and he told me I was beautiful and smart. He woke up emotions in my life that had no business being explored at my young age of thirteen. He was eventually caught and locked away for fifteen years after becoming involved with a close friend of mine at my school. Unlike me, she had two parents that were very involved and they found out she was skipping school to be with him.

Despite this setback, I graduated high school at sixteen years old. In the middle of my senior year, I went on to obtain a Medical Assisting degree at Sanford Brown College and maintained a 4.5 GPA. Although I never worked in this field, it was my desire to become a physician assistant or an RN.

Fast forward ... I am a mother of three beautiful girls: Zamaria, Mariaha, and Michelle who I named after my mom in remembrance of her. I'm currently married and building a career with the federal government. I have a cleaning service as well as a nonprofit organization in remembrance of my mom, to help other children like me and my brother.

I don't want another child or caregiver to experience the same hurt and the pain we endured while grieving the loss of my mother. I feel grief should not take forever. Me, my brother, and my grandmother only had grief counseling one time after losing my mother to domestic violence. As a result of this I became victim to other things, and my brother became the abuser and turned to the wrong people and crime to gain the love we always longed for from our mother. It's not that my brother was a horrible person or that I was this flirtatious, promiscuous young girl, we just lacked love, attention, guidance, and finances to help channel our pain in other positive directions.

I want this to stop, and I want to make people aware of this issue because this is becoming a bigger problem than just the event that transpired between my dad, Michael Grider, and my mom, Michelle Gadson. I want to be able to give caregivers a break and send them on a once-a-year retreat or vacation, even if it's just for

Breaking the Silence

a weekend because they are true living angels to the children that are left behind after mothers are killed by domestic violence.

I remember my grandmother having to suppress her grief by having a drink to fall asleep at night because of the worry of bills, Christmas, school shopping, repairs that needed to be done to our home, new appliances, repairs to the breaker box, plumbing, washing machine, car repairs, or the times we just needed a new car. Enduring all of this while grieving the loss of her daughter and taking care of her two grandchildren. Later she had to take custody of her nephew's sister because their mom was also murdered. No one should have to do this alone.

My dream is to create a team and a village that will rescue these types of children that are in the back yard of American people's homes. I even want to extend this to areas all over the world. This is not only a mission, but also a great passion of mine. I also want to teach children like myself how to forgive their fathers. They may not grow or create a bond like my father and I have, but they need to know forgiveness is for them, not their father or any other perpetrator. It is the key to your destiny and the power to your purpose. If you're wondering if you are reading right, yes you are. I have forgiven and I also have a remarkable curse-breaking relationship with my father. I love my father as if he had never done anything.

I like to hear my father greet me as "Beautiful" and tell me how much of a remarkable woman of God I am. How proud of me he is and how grateful he is for our relationship and how much power our testimony has been to so many people behind bars that he tries to help and minister about the ugly demon of domestic violence. I like to see the amazement on people's faces when they see me and my father during visitations. God is very much a living God because he lives inside of me. Although I am not perfect, the posture of my heart is correct and because my father is a born-again believer in Christ, our relationship literally gets stronger and stronger each year. I was twenty-eight when I decided to forgive my father and I have loved him ever since.

ABOUT THE AUTHOR

Tierra Carter, formerly known as Tierra Gadson, is the CEO and founder of Mother's Fighting from The Grave Inc. Tierra is an advocate for children and caregivers left behind after a child or children experience the trauma of losing their mother due to domestic violence. Tierra continues to work hard to build a nonprofit organization that will assist with the needs of these children as well as their caregivers. She became a founder of such an organization out of her own traumatic event of losing her mother at the young age of four from domestic violence. Tierra continues to work hard to build the organization through partnerships and speaking up about her experience through social media and countless other platforms.

Tierra hopes to bring more awareness to how children such as herself and her sibling and her caregiver her grandmother needed and lacked so many resources. These families will need mental, financial, and educational support. Support for extra activities as a form of outlet due to this trauma these are also great needs in communities across the world. This is a hidden issue that she desires to reveal through her organization to empower the voices of the mothers who continue to fight even beyond their graves. If you are interested in helping to build and even become a board member for this organization, please reach out to her via Instagram @MFGHOPE.

CHAPTER 20
COMPLEX

Wah Wah Tas See (Anonymous Author)

They call it "complex trauma." From the driver's seat, here's what it feels like: You get knocked down by a heavy blow, get up to your feet again, shake yourself off, take a few steps, and a blow from a different opponent you couldn't see knocks you over. You stay down for a minute, evaluate the surroundings, get back up, expect another blow. Nothing comes, you carry on. Before you know it, you have forgotten you were on the ground and hurt. Then a car runs a stop sign and plows into you. At that point, you are a survivor. Just figure it out. Now you not only have to watch for people, but for cars. Time goes by, things seem a little better, then betrayal. Terrible heartbreaking betrayal. Now you must learn to be ready for this as well. It feels like every time you try to get up, you get knocked back down. Then sometimes the attacker even lends you a hand and acts like it was no big deal, "Why are you upset about it?" Silly girl ...

What a life.

Other than the two repetitive death dreams I had as a child, all the rest were mostly running. Trying to escape, feeling trapped. I was always trying to figure out the plan and the strategy to get away from the bad guys, whoever they were. Complex trauma may not be the big bad wolf, but it is a corrosion of who you are and how you act on the deepest level. It is like a story where the plot isn't allowed time for rest and reflection. It continues to escalate, and the antagonist is fiercely relentless.

I was born to a couple fresh out of the hippie years. The picture of Dad holding me and smiling shows pure love ... a love I'm not sure I'll ever know again. When Mom held me, it was like being asked to hold someone's dog when you don't like dogs in general. She barely smiled, just a face of performing the duty that was expected of her. No joy, just a bland presence.

Two quick years passed, and my father was consumed with pain and suffering from cancer caused by exposure to asbestos and smoking. The cancer had spread everywhere by the time the doctors found it. It wrapped around his spine and invaded his brain. The medical world at the time had completely limited resources to manage cancer, and he died a terrible suffering death. I do not remember being allowed to say goodbye to him in his last weeks. This was the origin. The scale tipped, and for what felt like forever, pain, loss neglect, betrayal, death, abandonment, and on and on ... this was all I knew.

 Six months after his death, my mother was with a guy who was the opposite of my father, who was going to make money and take care of her. She wanted the lifestyle of social status and security. She did this without considering what that pathway would mean for her children, as two more were coming soon. A few years in, he adopted me, and the next thirty-five years would be full of ups and some very tremendous downs.

 Flash forward, I'm the step kid who's resented for being somewhat smart, or heaven forbid anyone said I was pretty. If compliments came my way, I knew later that day he'd be mocking me, putting me down, isolating me, harassing me. All of it. To this day I must work on accepting compliments. By twelve years old, the sexual inappropriateness was well under way: watching me in the bathtub exploring my body, dropping ice down the front of my bathing suit at a family pool party and saying I had nothing there to catch it, on and on. Sometimes I'd look in the mirror in my bedroom and see myself and how sad I was, and I'd cry. I realized I felt so alone and no one in this home cared, and I'd cry for myself as if I were looking at someone else and my heart was breaking for them. It was a strange feeling.

 My emotionally absent mother couldn't be bothered to teach me how to be a young woman and resented me deeply. I'll never understand where her pain stemmed from. I had to learn about my cycle from a girl I didn't know at a summer camp, and when I told my mom, she told me that because I used a tampon, I was a slut and must have had sex now. As I became an older teen, I was told all sorts of inappropriate stories from both of my parents. I can tell you how often their agreement was to have intercourse like a contract, I can tell you what song they listened to when it was fun for them, I can tell you how pathetic my dad thought it was that my mom wouldn't perform oral sex in the back of a limo, so many things. No boundaries were allowed. I didn't understand for decades how my lack of knowing what boundaries were or how to establish them affected me. This was the foundation for my intimate relationships going forward for many years.

My poor mother was insulted on a regular basis. She couldn't even wash her face at night for fear he would criticize what she looked like in the morning. It makes me sick the things he said to her and about her. Later in life I had to pull him aside after corporate meetings with a majority of women in leadership to explain that he can't talk about my mother in a derogatory way … or can't talk about women not saying no during rape because "It isn't that big a deal" and "Guys enjoy it when women take advantage of younger men."

My sibling and I would come down in the morning at home to be insulted and told we were going to get fat if we didn't be careful. We were told our assess would be bigger than a house. "Ugh, did you even wash your hair today?" was a classic. Of course I did, but I have very thin hair and a mother who didn't teach me to style it, so I did the best I could. When people kissed his ass, he'd greet them with an upward inflection and act happy to see them. What an exhausting way to live, to try to get loyalty and affection through constant manipulation and abuse.

A quick trauma blip outside the norm at this point: One normal afternoon an idiot teenage boy did something foolish, thinking he'd be funny and or a jerk. I ended up in the ICU for a traumatic head injury and a brain bleed. I will spare you the details. I fully recovered in the end.

However, after the head injury, I couldn't stand all this home drama and finally having had enough of the toxic, misogynistic household I ran away. I was fifteen. I went to a friend of a friend's house that night who kept giving me more and more vodka. My tiny body couldn't handle it. I ended up waking up for a moment on the couch with my pants off and him moving my limp body up to a different place on the couch that better served his efforts. I blacked out again. Betrayal … again.

Breaking the Silence

In the morning, my girlfriend and I stomped on his cowboy hat and trashed his room, then tried to figure out where we could go from there. He looked at me as we were leaving and laughed. He said, "What, do you think I raped you?" He laughed again. Fire burned in my soul.

I got the worst case of strep throat, and couldn't eat or drink, so I had to return home. My stepdad looked at me with such disgust and judgement and accusingly asked "Well, where are the torn underwear, huh?" I knew then I couldn't talk about being raped. I wasn't attacked in an alley by a stranger, so therefore it was something I must have asked for. I closed the door and buried it down until one of my angels came along. I'll call her "Penelope."

I was a public shame to my family, and sent to an out of state reform school. It was so bizarre and full of psychotic brainwashing, I had to leave. I put most of it behind me but remember bits and pieces. Screaming to depressing music in a room full of other troubled teens with tube socks over our arms beating pillows, only to have the counselors in this place sleeping with students and treating some with so much shame they made them dig holes in the ground only to refill them. They made one girl walk around with "Slut" on a big sign across her chest because she kissed a boy she had a crush on.

It was a mad house where betraying your friends was the expectation, gossip was common, and sick, controlling people were in power. The good counselors were few, but I gravitated to them and found safety. I believe it was where I first learned to trust again. I remembered I had a voice. As those people left, guess what I did? I ran. Forty miles in the snow with another friend only to get to town and have a bounty hunter slam us up against a car and take us to a holding place for the next place I was shipped to.

The woods. We carried our food, water, and supplies up and down the mountain every day. Four-minute showers, a small classroom mixed with kids ranging from eleven to eighteen years old. Penelope was there. I was very closed off about the rape after my stepdad's absolute botching of how to address your teenage daughter after a date rape. Penelope helped me. I wrote, I drew, I yelled, I cried. I joined a group for young girls who had been sexually abused and listened to their stories and supported them. My heart broke there. The wannabe cowboy slipped into my past, eventually fading away like a trivial piece of a story that doesn't even feel like mine.

Flash forward, I go home for senior year. My home is just as awful, if not more, and I do what? I run again. Seventeen years old. A new boyfriend's family was okay with me staying there. I finished high school on my own and got into college. I arrived to a massive state college and felt utterly lost and alone. I gravitated to old behaviors that felt safe. I partied. I passed some classes, failed a couple, but had zero direction.

One boyfriend got into cocaine, I didn't want that life, got away from him, and the rebound casual next thing became an "oops." I faced the surprise of a life and did the best I could. My deep south grandmother heard the father was Hispanic and made a disgusted face and said I had to get rid of it, like I had a filthy disease in me that needed to be irradicated. I hated that. Grandma did not have much couth. She could have sat and had a heart-to-heart with me, and it may have gone differently. Hindsight is always offering a different view.

My parents just said I should give him up for adoption, but then I feared he'd be in a home where he might be unloved. As the empath in the narcissist home, I was always the fixer and the peacemaker, so of course in my mind there was a high probability of him being unloved or mistreated. I never wanted him to feel the way I had.

I stayed the course thinking I could do this alone if I need to. Nine months passed and it was time to deliver ...

My son's umbilical cord is around his neck, my epidural had been patchy and ineffective. We are trying to power through. Forceps (which I previously requested we not use) are brought into play, I'm screaming, the doctor pulling and pulling, and it happens. My son's heart slows down and stops ... asystole. Everyone is in a dead panic. A hand is on my son's head and they are pushing him back inside me. While pushing him inside me, we are rolling down the hallway, panic everywhere. I'm signing papers I have no clue

Breaking the Silence

about, I'm on pain medicine, I'm terrified I'm losing my baby, I'm still laboring. We get to the OR and of course the extra medicine to the epidural isn't adequate. I feel like my insides are being ripped out of me, as if they sliced me open and were pulling out anything there—my uterus, my guts, everything ...

I'm sure my son was out within a matter of sixty seconds once we started, but who knows how long it took to get there. Once they had time to draw up meds, I was put under general anesthesia and didn't wake up for four hours after. Bonding was difficult. I was all alone. I don't know where my family or my son's dad was. I remember laying alone in this dark maternity room asking for pain meds. The baby in the basinet beside me, I hurt so bad, I couldn't breast feed. I was all alone. No one was there after this crazy situation where my son almost died, and I went through some level of hell. Postpartum depression is real. It is *dark* and it is scary. I am grateful that I don't remember the details of my thoughts anymore. I did the best I could to hold my baby, sing to my baby, and love my baby. In time, it got easier.

I tried to stay with the guy and had one other child before knowing he would never grow up and never love them or love being a husband. I left at five months pregnant. I was terrified. My family was so superficial, and it appeared like they really didn't like me, let alone love me, on a *real* level. I decided I never wanted to depend on anyone to take care of me, because up until this point, the people I was supposed to be able to trust the most had only ever betrayed me. So, I started the arduous task of being a single mom/student in a family with a detached mother and siblings that had run off to other states to avoid the home drama. What could go wrong? Who needs a loving support system as a young single mom trying to pursue a career? Ha!

Nothing I did was good enough. Criticized for even the food—eggs and sausage breakfast sandwiches to have a filling meal before school. Somehow, I was supposed to have the time and energy to be a gourmet chef as well. I was in survival mode. I tucked them in at night after reading their bedtime stories, then I studied for hours and hours. Barely getting any sleep, I'd get up early and go to classes or clinicals in the hospital units, mostly the

Breaking the Silence

ICUs. My mother would complain to her friends, "Ugh, I had to take care of my grandkids today." Always a burden, never a pleasure. My home was toxic, truly a sick place with alcoholism, cruelty, judgment, gaslighting, control. Plus, my kids' father did not have the capacity to love them.

    I tried to play the game; my kids were fine when we moved away. We had such beautiful years when they were young. So much fun, so much love. Cuddling, Friday night movie and pizza, hiking, day trips to Disney and the surrounding parks. They were the light of my life.

    Back home around the family, they learned to disrespect women from my stepdad, they learned complete disrespect for authority from my one sibling. Meanwhile, I took on a very advanced degree and pursued my dream job, hoping to show my children the benefit of hard work.

    My son who suffered the brain injury during birth developed a neurologic condition. So many specialists, so many doctor's appointments. He had a meltdown in middle school and said, "Mom, I'm so angry, please help me." I immediately withdrew from my program and lost all the front-loaded tuition. I took a normal nine-to-five to give him stability.

    Things got better, he felt like he was ready, and I was ready. I applied again and got in with the condition of, "This is the last shot." A semester in, things were going well, but the social pressures of school were affecting him. He hit puberty full on and it exacerbated insanely, aggravated by bullying in school. On Mother's Day, my son looked at me with such despair and said, "I don't want to live like this forever." I held him and he cried. His medications were hit or miss with severe side effects until we could get them under control. I did my best to stay strong and not let him see me scared. I would tuck them in at night and go to my bedroom, close the door, and cry so hard. I was the fixer who was completely unable to fix or help. He got better to some degree, but his acting out put him with the worst group of kids and drugs. His never-present father agreed to step in and try to help.

    Flash to the other side of my life as my sons were now with their father searching for male guidance. My concept of men and

Breaking the Silence

love is broken. I have only lived in narcissist environments, and even in my own home, when my children got older, it was the same. Gaslighting, stealing from me, lying to me, constantly betraying me. Being kind and praying on my love when they wanted something out of me, then stabbing me in the back. It was awful. I went through relationship after relationship trying to find what I missed in the last one. One betrayal after another. I've had guys break into my house after a breakup and put spyware on my computers. I've had guys get addicted to pain pills and quit work and just live off me for so long before I could finally get them out.

My mother did step up there. She helped me scrape off the bad men when it came time when I was younger. But when the "big bad" happened, my family let me down in ways I never could have imagined.

The big bad. I think my stepdad knew he was still married with kids. I don't know. Love bombing—it's a thing. Everything from date one was a con. I was so overwhelmed with all the love I'd never felt. So taken with this guy. He wasn't even attractive, but these guys know how to target a woman who has a hole in her heart and use that. Long story short, he did divorce his wife (there was endless drama there). He slowly isolated me from all my friends and family. He waited until vulnerable moments and got details out of me about my family, then used them to later convince me how bad they were. My family wasn't great, but it was my family and there was some good there. He sought to destroy that good.

I had only minimally studied domestic violence, but the pattern was textbook. Not only was he working me over financially, but he was also moving us into the most messed up experiential pattern of my life. The highs during the honeymoon phase were incredible, but the lows before the blowouts were insane. Eventually, I lived in fear. I feared what would trigger him. A picture of me with a friend or an old boyfriend, I better throw away that shirt. A TV show that makes him think about relationships and intimacy, I better change the channel or he'll get jealous and take it out on me.

Breaking the Silence

I destroyed so much of my history and belongings trying to avoid a fight with him. I realized what was happening to me and slowly pulled away. As I tried to pull away, he got more controlling. One night in a hotel, changing clothes, I was in my underwear and he was losing it. I tried to leave and he wouldn't let me have my clothes or get to the door. I locked myself in the bathroom and said, "If you don't let me go, I'm going to scream." Uncharacteristic of me, but I mustered up the courage and I screamed. I screamed a blood-curdling scream to hopefully get someone's attention to come help me.

NO ONE CAME!

He realized I was serious and tried to bring it back to kindness. I was getting dressed to leave. He went in the bathroom and wrapped a computer cord around his neck, and I heard a dramatic thud in the bathroom. I saw this cord not even remotely secure or possible of having choked him. I had to pretend everything was okay and go out with my friends and fake being happy. I was terrified. I look back and wish I had just understood that I could have found a way to get away from him, but at the time, I didn't believe it.

I was faking normalcy but now slowly trying to plan an exit. At one point, with his small children sleeping in the back seat, we were driving on the freeway, and I carefully started dropping hints of considering divorce. He lost his mind and tried to run us off the road, saying if he can't have me, no one can. I did everything in my power to reason with him and remind him of the innocents in the back seat. He said he'd rather them be dead than with his ex-wife. It took at least a year to finally leave.

My youngest son comes and goes with the drama always involved. I always try to keep my head above water. Talking to my one girlfriend who could understand the messed-up things I've gone through was all I had to keep my sanity. She and I sadly met odds a few years ago and I haven't seen her. I miss her. The day my ex lost his mind for the final time and took the phone so I couldn't call the police, he was killing small animals in the back yard. I locked myself in the bathroom, but he broke in. I feared he'd go outside and kill my pet to hurt me …

Breaking the Silence

CLICK.

Right there, I knew. Wake up! You care about everything else but yourself. HE MAY KILL YOU! I slept in another room that night and there would be no other night like this ever. My girlfriend played the psychology game with him on the phone for four hours the next day and got him to agree to leave the house. I changed the locks, called the police, and got a lawyer.

Even after feeling like I escaped, I found out he had stopped paying one credit card and my credit had dropped. I was overwhelmed with his debts. I agreed to take them all just to make him go away and make the divorce inevitably as fast as the law would allow. My girlfriend ran a background check on him and we found out he was a lifelong con artist. I won't go into the details, but this guy was bad. I was lucky to get away after just a few years.

This was the darkest period of my life. He completely shattered my relationship with my family. He brought up all the past I had let go of and made it fester and fester to where I went and confronted my family. They continued to armchair quarterback my parenting and judge me even though I love my children more than life itself. I couldn't take it anymore. I severed ties with them. I did it in a way that I wish I hadn't, but the darkness I was buried under was going to be the literal death of me. I was in absolute and utter survival mode. In one fail swoop, I lost my parents, my siblings and the icing on the cake was my children making bad choices including drug use and crime. As I scrambled to survive my own situation, they resented me for trying to hold them accountable for their choices. Eventually, it got worse and worse to a point of me having to completely detach from everything that I knew and loved. The reality was, I might be dead if I didn't.

Here is where things change. I finally learned what boundaries are. I had to set them at the expense of all the narcissistic relationships I had within my family, I had to set them with my abusive ex-husband, and I had to set them with my manipulative children who, at that time, only came around to use me, then hurt me and leave. The universe blessed me with a family of friends in the place I found myself for a few years while I

Breaking the Silence

healed. I can never express my gratitude and love for this group of people.

There were ups and downs, and I found myself in another imbalanced relationship where I was a caretaker for someone who didn't know how to love themselves or care for themselves. The imbalance was very unhealthy and draining. In time, I let it go. Boundary. At least there had been love here.

The next step was to move myself back to a less remote place where I could have rewarding work plus some normal life again. I fell into heavy work mode. I worked long days every day and went home, watched TV, and woke up to do it again. Completely sedentary. I was and am disappointed in myself, but it was a part of the process. After a year in a great job, where I almost stayed on in a very respectable role, I had to make a decision: comfort and security or push for actual thriving. I chose the push.

I moved back to my favorite city of all time. It took a year of ups and downs, but I started to exercise, I started to go to the theatre, I started to be more active with friends and not *just* work. I feel alive again. I feel a sense of strength and peace I have literally never known. The people who poisoned my daily life have no effect on me anymore. I surround myself with people who bring me up and balance me. Good people. Boundaries are a part of my daily life.

I took a chance and tried something new. Brazilian jiujitsu (I started slow with private lessons). My world was rocked. It was the perfect time for the perfect gift from the universe. My mind is engaged in a way I can't explain. When I'm in that space, I am fully present. The rest of the world melts away. My body is changing; the aging and stiffness is loosening up. My brain is excited. Truly inspired for the first time in many years, this is where my rebirth truly began. I've never felt more fulfilled.

There can be a light at the end of the tunnel if you let it. Keep putting one foot in front of the other. Be observant of what the universe is putting in front of you. There are lessons there. Be open to learning them, even the ones that are painful ... you can grow from them. Where there is a void, often predators want to enter, but also, angels may show up. Welcome the angels. I have had a few of the most beautiful angels come into my life in my difficult years that showed me the seeds of how to love myself.

    Penelope showed me how to forgive. How to let myself run the course of every emotion I needed to feel and let it all be expressed, so the energy could move on. She taught me accountability. My best friend's mother and father were and are like parents to me forever. I will be forever a better person from the love that people like Mama B and Papa B have shared with me. Let those people love you. The takers will always make themselves known. Then set your boundary and let them go, but don't be afraid to let the good people in. If I can give one bit of advice it's that life continues.

    When you start putting one foot in front of the other and pay attention to the direction of every step, you will most likely find yourself on an entirely different and better pathway down the road. Maintain hope, keep breathing, and get back up so you can find your footing again. The way to a life filled with light is there, it just takes many small steps to find it … and many more steps to really get where you want to go! Let your angels be there for you along the way. And when you can, be an angel for someone else.

EPILOGUE

Michelle Jewsbury

As we conclude our transformative journey through the pages of *Breaking the Silence: Voices of Survivors Vol. 2,* we may find ourselves faced with decisions about our own lives. Each of these stories have made an impactful difference, potentially inspiring us to take action and make meaningful change.

No matter your experience, your story has significant value. I often speak to individuals unaware that their courage to speak out has saved people's lives and impacted others to create a new path. Our life is our choice. We can choose to allow our adversities to define us or we can choose to define our experiences and use them for the betterment of the world. God has given us a mouth to speak, and we can be the changemakers on the planet.

It takes a collective to stop injustice. It takes boldness and courage to use our voices to stop generational cycles of trauma. It takes your voice for others to break free. Thank you for supporting our authors in their courageous act to speak up.

ABOUT THE AUTHOR

Michelle Jewsbury, a dynamic force in transforming personal stories into powerful narratives, is the founder and CEO of Unsilenced Voices. With a mission to empower survivors of adversity, Michelle has emerged as an internationally recognized speaker, coach, and advocate. Renowned for her expertise in translating adversity into business and personal success, she has graced stages across the globe. From sharing her journey of breaking the cycle of abuse, Michelle inspires individuals to transform their own stories into impactful narratives. As the driving force behind Unsilenced Voices, Michelle Jewsbury is dedicated to engaging individuals to harness the transformative power of their stories. Michelle Jewsbury can be seen on ABC, NBC, CBS, FOX, PBS, and more. You can reach her at MichelleJewsbury.com and UnsilencedVoices.org.

Breaking the Silence

To schedule a call and download a complimentary gift, please visit www.MichelleJewsbury.com

Made in the USA
Columbia, SC
12 October 2024